Advanced
Questionnaire
Design

Advanced Questionnaire Design

Patricia J. Labaw

Abt Books, Cambridge, Massachusetts

Library of Congress Cataloging in Publication Data

Labaw, Patricia J., 1937-
    Advanced questionnaire design.

    Bibliography: p.
    Includes index.
    1. Questionnaires. 2. Public opinion polls.
3. Social science research. I. Title.
HM261.L13 1981   303.3'8   80-69665
ISBN 0-89011-553-2   AACR2

Printed in the United States of America

Distributed by, Ballinger Publishing Company.

Contents

Preface

I regard this book as an extension and expansion of issues covered in Stanley Payne's *The Art of Asking Questions*. In his preface to that book, Payne not only describes his own qualifications and goals, but basically he describes mine also. I too write as a general practitioner of research, not as a specialist or an expert in semantics.

However, Mr. Payne quite plainly states that his book "discusses the wording of single questions almost exclusively. It hardly touches upon problems of question sequence or the overall matter of questionnaire design." Where Mr. Payne stops, this book begins. I limit my discussion of individual question wording in order to concentrate on problems of overall questionnaire design.

Although I've tried to be explicit, the reader will not find a definite set of rules or detailed instructions for writing a questionnaire. Each questionnaire is different, and thus each presents its own unique set of problems. However, I have tried to give concrete examples from a variety of studies of problems and possible solutions to those problems. Nevertheless, questionnaire design is an art and takes an artist's subjectivity and sensitivity to be successful. The effort is repaid in an expanded understanding of human nature, which I continue to find the ultimate reward and joy of my profession.

In this book I have often not presented the detailed statistical results from the questions used as examples. I have been constrained by the confidentiality of those data, which are still owned by the clients who paid for them. Wherever possible, however, I have presented results to support my arguments. As you begin to implement some of the suggestions outlined in this book, you will obtain your own data supporting or perhaps questioning my contentions.

I am a practitioner and have obviously written this book from that perspective, with considerable emphasis on the needs of the client relationship. Nonetheless, I believe the book will prove as valuable to academicians in the field, buyers of survey research, and other users of surveys as it will to those engaged in survey research as their primary vocation.

I am indebted to numerous colleagues from whom I learned the tools of my trade and with whom I endlessly discussed the unfathomable aberrations in the "data," trying to understand "what happened." I am particularly indebted to my colleague and business partner, Michael A. Rappeport, for his creative tabulation and data-processing designs, which supported our investigations into why some questions worked and others did not, why answers varied by subgroups, and what this variation meant to our data. Without his patience and his healthy skepticism about sampling precision as the answer to all survey problems, this book and its ideas would never have come into the open.

Patricia J. Labaw
Princeton, New Jersey
July 1980

Introduction

Public opinion polling has become ubiquitous. It has progressed from a curiosity to a major industry with its own professional association. In all major areas affecting individual lives in the United States, the results obtained from public opinion polls are determining public policy.

On the national level, polling determines which candidates will run for presidential office. A slide in the president's popularity, as measured by public opinion polls, makes him appear vulnerable and encourages both Republican and Democratic contenders to challenge him for reelection. The gradual but constant growth in the number of people opposed to U.S. involvement in Vietnam, once again measured by periodic opinion polls, ultimately forced Lyndon Johnson to relinquish a second term in office.

Outside the political arena, experiments in the design, delivery, and administration of various social service programs, such as minimum family income, urban redevelopment, child care services, and nutritional programs for the elderly, are based on polls among potentially eligible respondents to ascertain attitudes and to define possible roadblocks to effective use of services. Additional polling is conducted to obtain indications of public support for such programs in order to intercept backlash or to direct public relations efforts.

On the state level, to receive Title XX funds for social services, such as mental health care, family planning, transportation, alcohol treatment, counseling, or day care, each state must submit to the U.S. Department of Health and Human Services a plan showing priorities for distribution of the funds among the different Title XX programs. In many states these priorities are set as a result of statewide public opinion polls that attempt to measure levels of need for specific services by key subgroups, such as the elderly, minorities, single heads of household with children, inner city residents, and rural residents.

Incumbent and aspiring politicians use polling to identify major issues of concern to constituents and to plot the themes to use in TV commercials, newspaper advertising, and direct mail leaflets. Polling tells the candidate what issues not to discuss, how to discuss those issues he does raise, and those neighborhoods where he should spend most of his time versus those he should absolutely avoid.

Major banks, as part of their introduction of new financial services, poll their customers to determine levels of antagonism or favorability toward the proposed services, to identify the best procedures to use in the introduction of the services, and to help design the advertising which will accompany them.

Fast food restaurants conduct continuing market research to test what kinds of menus they should use to attract more breakfast customers, what types of customers most frequently use fast food restaurants, and how these subgroups are growing or declining as a proportion of the total U.S. population.

A major bank, under a consent decree to equalize its hiring and promotion policies, conducts a complete employee census to determine whether employees are aware of the new hiring procedures, whether these procedures are in fact working correctly, and how much confidence employees place in the procedures as a remedy for past inequities. The poll also investigates how well management's communications about corporate policy and goals are reaching the employees and what types of information workers want and need to improve their on-the-job performance.

On a local level, polls are conducted among town residents to determine attitudes toward services available in the town, for example, satisfaction with trash pickup, the condition of the roads, and the quality of the schools. A county polls its residents to learn how they feel about sex education in the schools, what facilities should be improved, whether new buildings should be constructed or whether they should redistrict to improve the use of existing buildings, whether they should introduce more vocational education courses or emphasize college preparatory skills.

Why the increase in polling?

The increasing use of polling derives both from greater need and greater opportunity. The need arises from a universal problem: limited resources and unlimited desires. The U.S. government has this problem; so do corporations and other levels of government. Priorities must be set for the spending of available money. Moreover, the immense increase in institutional size and complexity has made the problems themselves difficult to define and less amenable to intuitive solutions. Rather than risk their own necks on a seat-of-the-pants decision, managers, executives, and politicians now use polls to help them gain greater understanding of the issues, alternatives, and future impacts of their decisions. Polling has become one of the primary tools used to define goals and set priorities.

The opportunity arises because the United States, as one of the most completely developed countries in the world, supports an infrastructure that makes feasible cheap and extensive public opinion polling. We have an expert, constantly active Bureau of the Census that provides the data on population growth, changes, location, and demographics to enable projectable national probability samples to be drawn. The United States has the highest incidence of working telephones in the world, which allows telephone polling even in the most rural and isolated areas of the country. National television provides a common level of information and a common market across the country, which produces homogeneity of tastes and behavior. The huge growth in data-processing equipment enables researchers to gather and process masses of numbers and quantities of variables that were impossible to analyze twenty years ago. Mandatory universal education has brought the total populace to a minimum level of competency in understanding and speaking English, despite variations in regional accents and regional interpretations of words. Thus, the need to set priorities, combined with this massive technical infrastructure, creates a favorable climate for continued growth in public opinion polling and the questionnaires that provide the foundation for every poll.

□ 1
The layers of a questionnaire

Everybody understands that words go into questions and that questions go into questionnaires. What people do not understand is that writing questions does not give you a questionnaire. A questionnaire is *not* simply a series of questions, nor is a question merely a series of words.

A questionnaire is a structure consisting of several different layers, or facets, each one of which must be considered individually, but each one of which must then be integrated into the final instrument to form a completed questionnaire. This book is a discussion of these layers: what they are and what they mean to the total questionnaire design.

Layer 1—words

This is the most readily accessible level of questionnaire design, and also the one most often discussed in textbooks of survey research methods.

Wording problems include ambiguity of words, discrete versus multiple meanings of words, words as they embody concepts, culturally derived meanings of words, complex meanings which make words too difficult for the average respondent to understand, and technical or "jargon" words in common parlance among professionals but not commonly understood or used by other groups of people.

Words color and guide respondent answers. Examples of words that strongly affect the direction of respondent answers are "might, could, should," and "you":[1]

1) "Do you think anything *should* be done to make it easier for people to pay doctor or hospital bills?"

2) "Do you think anything *could* be done to make it easier for people to pay doctor or hospital bills?"

3) "Do you think anything *might* be done to make it easier for people to pay doctor or hospital bills?"

When conducting studies of the use of financial services, if the interviewer asks, "How many savings accounts do you have?", the respondent can (or might or should) wonder, does the interviewer mean just the savings account I have in my own name, the savings account I have jointly with my husband, or the savings accounts the household has, including those of each of the children? "You" in the English language carries both singular and plural meanings, and failure to distinguish between "you personally" and "your household or family" can either understate or overstate the incidence of service use.

Wording changes make a difference in polling results when they change the meaning of questions. In an article entitled, "The Polls: Polling on Panama—Si; Don't Know; Hell, No!", Bernard Roshco discusses the various polling efforts made prior to and after the Panama Canal treaty debates in the Senate.[2] As an aside in his article, Roshco writes, "The stability of pro-treaty responses (at approximately the twenty-nine percent level) and of anti-treaty responses (at approximately the fifty-three percent level) across diverse questions put by different pollsters is one of the most interesting trends the data reveal." Roshco lists the following series of questions, showing wide differences in question wording but very stable results: a situation that runs counter to conventional polling wisdom, which emphasizes the need for continuity in wording to measure trends.

Do you agree or disagree with the statement that our govern-

1. Stanley Payne, *The Art of Asking Questions* (Princeton, N.J.: Princeton University Press, 1951), pp. 8–9.
2. Bernard Roshco, "The Polls: Polling on Panama—Si; Don't Know; Hell, No!", *Public Opinion Quarterly*, Winter 1978.

ment should eventually return control of the Panama Canal to the government of Panama? (CBS, May 1976)

Agree	24%
Disagree	52
Undecided	24

Do you think the time has come for us to modify our Panama Canal Treaty or that we should insist on keeping the treaty as originally signed? (Roper, January 1977)

For modification	24%
Against	53
Undecided	23

Do you favor or oppose giving the Panama Canal back to the Panamanians even if we maintain our right to defend it? (Yankelovich, March 1977)

For giving back	29%
For holding on to it	53
Undecided	18

Do you think the United States should negotiate a treaty with Panama where, over a period of time, Panama will eventually own and run the Canal? (Caddell, May 1977)

Should negotiate	27%
Should not negotiate	51
Undecided	22

The Senate now has to debate the treaties that President Carter signed granting control of the Panama Canal to the Republic of Panama in the year 2000. Do you approve or disapprove of those treaties? (CBS, January 1978)

Approve	29%
Disapprove	51
No opinion	20

Even after the Senate approved the treaties, public opinion on the issues remained essentially the same as prior to ratification:

All in all, do you favor or oppose the treaties on the Panama Canal passed by the U.S. Senate? (Harris, June 1978)

Favor	35%
Oppose	49
Not sure	16

Do you think the Senate should have approved the Panama Canal treaties, or should not have approved them? (Roper, June 1978)

Should have approved	30%
Should not	52
Don't know	18

During the course of the extensive polling conducted prior to, during, and after the treaty ratifications, some pollers introduced a new issue into their questionnaires which resulted in a *complete reversal* of public approval of the Panama Canal treaties—the idea of U.S. intervention if necessary to our national security:

Would you favor or oppose approval of the Panama Canal Treaty if an amendment were added, specifically giving the United States the right to intervene if the Canal is threatened by attack? (NBC, January 1978)

Favor revised treaty	65%
Oppose	25

A poll conducted by CBS in October 1977 also found 63 percent approval and 24 percent disapproval when the issue of being able to send in U.S. troops was introduced.

The above series of questions, which include a wide range of wording variations, raises one of the fundamental tenets of this book: that question wording variations per se generally have little impact upon the stability of survey results. In other words, if the same basic concept, overall approval or disapproval of the Canal Treaties, for example, is being measured, minor variations in wording will have no effect on respondent answers.

Question wording variations become significant in survey results primarily when the variations introduce or tap a different concept or reality or emotional level surrounding an issue. Thus, when the questions on the Panama Canal treaties introduced the issue of U.S. intervention rather than mere overall approval or disapproval, an entirely different level of respondent reality or meaning was reached. Introduction of the factor of national security and troop intervention presented a different context or scenario which resulted in a radical change in opinion, although this change was not inconsistent or irrational. The words used were merely the vehicle for introducing this new concept to respondents, rather than the actual cause of respondent changes in answers. Yet variations in question wording unrelated to concept distinctions and specific formats of questions comprise the essential discussion in most books purporting to set forth principles of questionnaire design.

Layer 2—questions

The authors of standard texts on principles of survey research raise issues of question reliability, validity, and bias. They discuss questions in isolation from each other except for some special issues, such as position effect. They categorize individual questions on the basis of whether they are questions that deal with facts, beliefs, feelings, standards, actions, or behavior, or with conscious reasons for behavior or beliefs. They describe questions in terms of their format: are they open-ended or closed? Do the answer categories form a scale? Are the answer categories mutually exclusive? Is the respondent presented with all possible answer categories? Are the alternatives stated rather than simply implied?

These issues of definition are not important to questionnaire design, and, in fact, some of these issues of definition become very murky, such as the borderline between questions of feeling and questions of belief or attitudes. Basically, only two issues of importance relate to the questions themselves:

1) The type of question (open-ended or closed).
2) The quality of the question (good or bad).

In this book I will discuss two types of open-ended questions (completely open-ended and open with precoded answer categories) and closed questions, including the advantages and disadvantages of each type. I will also define two categories of questions: knowledge questions and behavior questions. Any other categories of questions provide little insight into the issues discussed in the remainder of this book. For a discussion of the other types of questions and the problems of their formulation, I refer the reader to any comprehensive book on survey methodology, but particularly to *The Art of Asking Questions*, by Stanley Payne.[3]

3. Stanley Payne, *The Art of Asking Questions* (Princeton, N.J.: Princeton University Press, 1951).

Examples of bad questions are those that are:

1) Incomprehensible to the respondent because either the wording, the concepts, or both cannot be understood by the respondent.

2) Unanswerable, either because the respondent does not have access to the information to enable him to answer it, or because the options provided as answer categories do not adequately encompass the true answer as perceived by the respondent.

3) Leading, in that the respondent is forced or directed into an answer that he would not ordinarily give if all possible answer categories or concepts were provided, or if all the facts of the situation were provided.

Bad questions are any questions that obscure, prohibit, or distort the fundamental communication from respondent to researcher. Notice the emphasis here—from respondent to researcher. A researcher may think he has written an excellent question because it accurately conveys his point of view or interest to the respondent, but if the respondent cannot answer it meaningfully, it still remains a bad question.

Layer 3—format

The third layer of questionnaire design consists of the format or layout. Questionnaires are formatted to meet the demands of:

1) Obtaining accurate respondent meaning (asking multiple questions per topic and putting questions within the questionnaire into some orderly sequence to avoid position bias). An obvious example is that a questionnaire discussing nuclear power plants should not contain a series of questions at the beginning on radioactive waste disposal, nuclear accident, radioactivity emissions, and so forth, and then at the end ask the respondent to evaluate the safety of nuclear power plants compared with other forms of power generation. After the priming on the dangers of nuclear power, the respondent cannot be expected to give an objective answer that truly represents his feelings on the subject beyond that particular moment of the interview.

2) Providing smooth flow and modulated transitions throughout the interview from topic to topic. Generally, interviews

begin with rather broad or generalized topics and questions to lead the respondent gradually into the main topic of concern without too great a jolt. For example, on a bank marketing questionnaire it would not be wise to begin the interview with detailed questions about savings account balances, checking account balances, and family income, and then turn immediately to the respondent's attitudes toward different types of savings accounts. In this case, the respondent would be very likely to terminate the interview because of all the personal questions up front. Problems of modulated transitions become particularly important in the "omnibus" or multiple client questionnaires fielded periodically by many research firms. In this type of study a wide range of questions—from feminine hygiene products, to attitudes toward plastic furniture to attitudes toward travel to Japan—can all be included on one questionnaire.

3) Aiding the interviewer in following the branching, exclusions, and sequence of questions incorporated into the questionnaire. This is one aspect of formatting which I believe is frequently ignored by survey researchers, simply because they have never been forced into the field to conduct ten or fifteen forty-five-minute interviews themselves. Thus, they have not been faced with the serious difficulties posed by complex branching, routing, and the constant need to refer back to preceding pages to identify which part of the questionnaire should be administered next. Clean formatting of questionnaires to prevent interviewer error and thus speed the entire interviewing process can result in both much cleaner data and much lower cost.

In this regard, I try *never* to ask the interviewer to refer back to preceding pages to identify the next direction to follow in the interview. Furthermore, I virtually never provide interviewer instructions for the questionnaire which would require the interviewer to refer to them on the side during the interview. A questionnaire should be so clearly formatted that interviewer instructions, except for a few exclusion directions, are virtually not needed. I know from personal experience that interviewer supervisors and interviewers work most conscientiously on questionnaires that are easy to follow and administer.

4) Providing a fast punching format for accurate tabulation of the data. The main task here is to consult with your keypunching personnel on the format *before* the questionnaire is fielded to

insure that all of your punch categories make sense and can be found by the keypunchers. One important aspect of the punching format is that it subsequently meet the data needs of the survey researcher. Sometimes questionnaires are formatted so poorly that, although the data appear to be available, it becomes very costly to draw them off the questionnaire. Anticipation by the researcher of what types of cross-tabulations he will need, what types of scales he may wish to construct, and what types of cluster analyses he may use leads to a more logical and professional tabulation layout of the questionnaire.

In this book I discuss formatting specifically only in the context of obtaining respondent meaning from questions. I do not discuss formatting in other contexts, since styles of formatting are developed by each individual survey research firm and they tend to reflect the predominant type of survey conducted by each firm, such as consumer product marketing, government evaluation studies, social issues research, and political research. However, survey research costs can be lowered substantially by careful attention to formatting to aid rather than hinder the interviewer's progress through the questionnaire, and to aid efficient punching and tabulation of the data after the questionnaire has been returned from the field.

I have included in the summary chapter four pages of a typical questionnaire format I regularly use. It has been derived from the format standard used at Opinion Research Corporation for the ten years that I worked there. More importantly, I have had many interviewers and supervisors tell me that this format makes the interview a much easier and much more efficient process.

Layer 4—hypotheses

The preceding layers of questionnaire design are the material commonly covered in books discussing survey methodologies. The fourth layer of questionnaire design, that of hypothesis development, may be touched upon, but it is not usually presented in the same detail that I present it here. The concept of questionnaires as instruments for gathering meaningful data to test *hypotheses* (rather than merely to gather facts) is only implicit in most survey texts, and the idea that a questionnaire as a totality serves a research function for hypothesis testing aside from the questions it contains is often not discussed.

Although it is not obvious, when a survey researcher writes a questionnaire, he constructs it on the basis of certain hypotheses he holds, whether he is aware of them or not. Among these are hypotheses regarding:

1) The nature of the respondent.

2) The relationship between the expressed attitudes and behavior of the respondent (motivation).

3) The goals and needs of the client.

4) Sociological structures and their influence on the respondent.

5) The meaning of words and the respondent's grasp of language.

6) The relationships among knowledge, attitudes, and behavior.

A major emphasis in this book concerns the development of research hypotheses and the implications of these other unexamined yet assumed hypotheses upon the research process. The final layer of questionnaire design consists of conscious development of the hypotheses to be tested and their incorporation into the questionnaire through words, questions, and format.

Although I have listed the four major layers of questionnaire design from words to hypotheses in my discussion above, I have reversed the ordering of layers in the remainder of this book, beginning with hypotheses and ending with words. Hypothesis development, not wording, is the starting point of all questionnaires. You cannot begin to formulate questions and worry about wording unless you know what you want to accomplish with your questions and words.

The relationship between questionnaires and respondents

The final consideration in questionnaire design concerns the relationship between the researcher and the respondent. A questionnaire provides a means of communication, and the starting point for all questionnaire design is concern for and identification with the respondent in order to provide the means for a dialogue rather than a monologue. Thus, the respondent will define the types of questions you can realistically ask, the types of words you can reasonably use, the concepts you can explore, and the methodology you can use.

Questionnaire design resembles some procedures and rules of social anthropology. In a very real sense, questionnaires attempt a comparative study of different cultures through which we see similarities and differences in behavior and values, although the cultures reside as subgroups within the United States. As Margaret Mead explains in her preface to Ruth Benedict's *Patterns of Culture*, Benedict was concerned with "the relationship between each human being, with a specific hereditary endowment and particular life history, and the culture in which he or she lived."[4] Benedict herself defines anthropology as "the study of human beings as creatures of society."[5] Surely this is essentially the task and goal underlying most questionnaires administered in our society.

An important distinction between anthropology and other social sciences is that anthropologists urge the "informants" to speak of the meaning and purpose of their behavior. Moreover, the major occupational hazard of an anthropologist consists of viewing an alien culture through his own culture-conditioned eyes with a subsequent bias or distortion in his interpretation of the meaning of what he has observed in the other culture. To quote Benedict, "No man ever looks at the world with pristine eyes. He sees it edited by a definite set of customs and institutions and ways of thinking. His very concepts of the true and the false will still have reference to his particular traditional customs."[6]

Benedict goes on to explain that anthropology as a science was not even possible until European man began to stop seeing himself as absolutely unique when compared to other societies, when he stopped identifying his own ways of behaving as "Behavior" and his own socialized habits as "Human Nature."

In short, the goal of this book is to lay out methods of questionnaire design and mental attitudes which incorporate these two rules of anthropology:

4. Ruth Benedict, *Patterns of Culture*, Sentry Edition (Boston: Houghton Mifflin, 1961), p. ix.
5. Ibid., p. 2.
6. Ibid., p. 2.

1) Let the informant (or respondent) tell you what he means, what his life and values mean.

2) Design the questionnaire to prevent its becoming simply an instrument of the writer's perceptions, values, and language, which is then inflicted upon the respondent.

Corollaries of these two rules are that although we all speak English, we do not use our words the same ways, and we attribute different meanings or emphases to words depending upon our own cultural use of language. We may all behave in similar ways, but the motivations for that behavior often vary according to our own cultural habitat and its values. Conversely, we are all human beings with vast areas of common conduct and needs, so that differences between groups may be more apparent than real.

We can begin to understand these complexities only if we view a questionnaire as an instrument of *communication,* a two-way conversation between the respondent and the survey researcher. All of the techniques outlined in this book attempt to open the gates of communication to allow the *meaning* of words, behavior, and perceptions to come through from respondent to researcher and vice versa. In addition, the methods and techniques outlined in this book are designed to help keep the researcher objective, to help him avoid inflicting his own values and perceptions on the respondent and then subsequently saying that this is what the respondent actually meant.

☐ 2
What a questionnaire is and is not

A questionnaire is a gestalt

One definition of questionnaire, provided by the *American Heritage Dictionary of the English Language,* points up the underlying problem with the current state of the art in questionnaire design. The dictionary definition is: "A printed form containing a set of questions, especially one addressed to a statistically significant number of subjects by way of gathering information, as for a survey."

Notice that even here, in a definition of *questionnaire,* the sampling and statistical significance are emphasized. Sampling is what researchers and their clients scrutinize for possible "error" or "bias" of results, with only a passing glance at error in questionnaire design, which can falsify the results more thoroughly than any fraction of sampling error.

The dictionary definition of a questionnaire is hopelessly incomplete. A questionnaire is much more than a set of questions. It is a totality, a gestalt that is greater than the sum of its individual questions. A questionnaire is organic, with each part vital to every other part, and all parts must be handled simultaneously to create this whole instrument.

A questionnaire resembles a painting in its handling and development. While a painting consists of such components as lines, lights and darks, forms, composition, colors, and actual application of the paint, the artist cannot use a step-by-step sequence, handling one component entirely, followed by the next. All the components must be integrated and handled simultaneously, for if the artist becomes too preoccupied with a specific color, for example, the composition or balance of the painting will be skewed. Similarly, the color may overshadow the delicacy of the forms or obliterate the subtlety of the line. A painting in its totality conveys more than the individual parts, and so does a good questionnaire. While art educators attempt to interpret a painting by discussing its line, its chiaroscuro, and its composition, these individual components really explain nothing to the viewer about the inherent beauty of a Botticelli Venus, a Rembrandt self-portrait, or a Van Gogh sunflower.

Similarly, to explain only the individual components of a questionnaire—closed versus open-ended questions, dichotomous versus multiple choice, implied alternatives, scaling techniques—is to fail to understand or anticipate the impact of the total questionnaire structure on the search for meaningful results. This book will concentrate on the use of this total structure or gestalt in understanding the respondent's conceptual structure and the meaning of his answers.

A questionnaire is not a place to cut the budget

During the development phase of a survey, the questionnaire becomes many other objects in the minds of the researchers and the client. Questionnaires often bear the brunt of political, economic, and social pressures aroused during the development and implementation of a survey. Because questionnaires appear to be so fluid, so imprecise compared to samples, for example, compromises are more likely to occur here than in other parts of the overall project.

It is axiomatic in the survey research business that the greatest proportion of *controllable* costs lies in the interviewing phase. Thus, while on a theoretical level questionnaires are supposed to be written to gain a true picture of respondent reality, in practice questionnaires are often written in response to cost pressures, with the result that respondents are not allowed to tell you about reality as they perceive it. Questionnaires are shortened; interviews are transformed from in-person to telephone or to self-administered mailed forms to cut costs. Free-response questions are eliminated and replaced by closed-end questions with answer categories concocted by the researcher. The questionnaire is designed to provide a format that only keypunchers can readily follow to facilitate punching and tabulation of the data, ignoring the impact of this format on respondent answers. All of these actions may be necessary because of cost constraints or, as we shall see, may even be desirable for other reasons, but too often questionnaires are designed with these cost goals in mind rather than the goal of probing the respondent's mind and behavior.

Because a good questionnaire is conceived of and written as an integrated whole, it is virtually impossible to delete questions randomly without destroying the integrity of the instrument. After several cuts by committees of clients, the rationale behind the questionnaire may be so ravaged that the questionnaire ceases to function as an instrument and becomes only a series of sporadic shots at data collection. Its usefulness as a research tool, as a means of communication between respondent and researcher, and its final utility in producing data for meaningful analysis become so diluted, so incoherent, that the entire purpose of the project is undermined.

A questionnaire is not a political football

In addition to cost considerations, questionnaires are often designed in response to the politics surrounding the study itself. Because they are written in English (I use the term advisedly), questionnaires can become political instruments more easily and are more subject to political strife than any other phase of a project, except perhaps the interpretation of the data. Because there are no hard and fast rules governing questionnaire design, the researcher cannot defend his questionnaire against political sharpshooting in the same way he can defend his sample. A typical example of political controversy affecting questionnaire wording is the following: "This is a Catholic state. We cannot use the words 'birth control' in this questionnaire. We must use 'family planning.'"

As a result of this stricture, actual use of family planning in households was severely underreported, based on other available data used for comparison. Citizens of the state obviously do not regard "family planning" and "birth control" as synonyms. In fact, in a later study, when people were asked to define the meaning of the phrase "family planning," a considerable number defined it as budgeting for the future and financial management. This definition was also more often given by male respondents than female respondents.

Other examples of political problems are:

> Please don't use the question, "How old are you?" in this questionnaire. My boss thinks it's too blunt. Can't we ask something along the lines of, "Could I ask you how old you are?" [Yes, you can, but the respondent will probably simply answer, "No," and then where does that leave you?]

> We have a large Spanish population in this state and a Spanish member on our advisory board, so we've got to ask about bilozaria [schistosomiasis] and whether they use the services of a spiritualist for counseling help.

> I don't want to spend any time on this banking survey asking people whether they want this service or not. Management decided four years ago to go ahead with it, and we've already spent several million dollars on data-processing equipment, so we are going to do it whether they like it or not. Just concentrate on how well customers like this type of statement or that type, this type of check register or that type, colors, and whether they want to list their balance figures horizontally or vertically.

To argue effectively against arbitrary and capricious gutting of questionnaires for budgetary and political reasons, the researcher must be able to justify his individual questions and his entire questionnaire in terms of a systematic theory of questionnaire design with as much strength and validity as the theory backing up the sampling experts. One purpose of this book is to provide the foundation for such a theory, to provide a more systematic approach to questionnaire design beyond issues affecting individual words or individual questions.

A questionnaire is designed around systematic, theoretic principles

The great weakness of questionnaire design is lack of theory. A theory of questionnaire design of necessity begins to deal with a theory of human nature, and this leads to veritable tar pits of sticky problems. Stanley Payne's *The Art of Asking Questions* is still a basic work in the field, although written in 1951. His book and derivatives of it concentrate on problems of wording and types of questions, while giving some passing attention to format and to problems of position effects within the total questionnaire. However, he and others do not deal with a questionnaire as a means of predicting behavior, which leads into issues of human nature: psychology, attitude, and behavior. Certainly, no overall theory or systematic approach to questionnaire design is presented, nothing comparable to the body of sampling theory that now exists to guide survey design. This lack of theory is glaring when texts on survey design or methods are examined. By far the bulk of any such text in the field concentrates on sampling and techniques of data analysis, areas replete with theory.

Early in his book Stanley Payne emphasizes that writing a questionnaire is an art, not a science, a view I strongly endorse. Nonetheless, artists are trained. They do not just happen. They are educated in theories of art, technique, and aesthetics. Survey researchers are also trained, and the goal of this book is to begin to train them to increase the predictability of the data they gather using questionnaires by designing questionnaires systematically around some basic principles of human nature as it responds to the interviewing format.

A questionnaire is either descriptive or predictive

Two issues that affect the theory of questionnaire design concern the distinction between accuracy and precision in survey research, and descriptive versus predictive research projects.

While a questionnaire can combine both approaches, generally surveys are designed to be either descriptive or predictive. The

U.S. Census is an example of a descriptive or fact-finding study. Studies conducted by the U.S. Department of Energy simply to find out how many miles people drive their cars each day or at what temperature their thermostats are set are also descriptive and fact finding.

The distinction between the two types of surveys can often be seen in the titles applied to them. Fact-finding studies usually have static titles: "The Incidence of Use of Hospital Services," "Travel Habits of the U.S. Public," "Current Use of Financial Services." Policymaking projects, on the other hand, often contain active verbs in their titles which imply or specifically state that some action will be taken or behavior predicted as a result of the study: "An Evaluation of the Nutrition Project Among the Elderly," "Bank Customers React to a New Savings Service," "Potential Students Outline Educational Needs."

Whether we choose to recognize it or not, our society is basically marketing oriented. None of our institutions exists indefinitely on public sufferance; each must perform. Each must respond to need. As a consequence, every policymaker must know what the need is and try to learn the best way of providing the service or product to meet the need. The days of seat-of-the-pants decision making are passing, if they have not indeed already passed. This is true especially for the large corporations and government organizations now closely scrutinized for responsiveness to the needs of society in such areas as civil rights, employment, and the environment. When competing organizations struggle for public support and limited tax dollars, they have to be able to sell their positions both to the public that supports them and to their immediate superiors. Polling provides a major means of documenting their positions and types of needs. Thus, most studies now go beyond mere description and are commissioned to provide actionable policymaking information. This means prediction of human behavior under altered circumstances.

This book deals primarily with the research problems posed by a *predictive* survey questionnaire. We are interested in predicting behavior when conditions change. However, attitudes change when conditions change. Therefore, current attitudes cannot be used to predict future behavior. This is the research problem at the heart of predicting behavior from polls. We can't wait to see what will actually happen, so we try to construct the situation or scenario in advance and ask people to respond to it. The questionnaire is the tool used to construct this scenario in advance, and the extent to which we can accurately construct this picture and enable the respondent to react and express his reactions to it determines the accuracy with which we can then predict behavior.

A questionnaire should be accurate rather than precise

Another factor which often leads to poor questionnaire design is a preoccupation with precision rather than accuracy. Accuracy in questionnaire design can be defined as obtaining a true report of the respondent's position. Obtaining an accurate understanding of the respondent's position allows the researcher to predict behavior and attitude with greater consistency. Data are accurate when they provide a description of the true state of affairs. For data to give an accurate picture, questions must be constructed to obtain a total picture rather than a fragment.

Precision, on the other hand, has to do with the reproducibility of the results. A census, by definition, gives total precision. However, if the questions asked do not deal with respondent reality, a survey can be completely reproducible but give false results.

One example of misplaced precision in questionnaire design occurs when attitudes or behaviors are being tracked over long periods of time. Gradually, the questions used to measure the attitudes or behaviors become dated in their relevance, meaning, or even vocabulary. After a few years, such questions can end up eliciting meaningless information. The studies are very precise but very inaccurate.

Similarly, while a client or a researcher would rarely dream of lopping off one quadrant of a national sample, these same people will often delete an offensive question or one that they regard as too expensive without any sense at all of what this may do to the study's accuracy. In fact, good samples may give great precision, but they may or may not affect a study's accuracy. Precision should not be the determining factor in a survey design. Precision is a concept more applicable to the physical sciences, while accuracy is a concept more in harmony with the social sciences.

What is in people's minds, and how do we find it?

O, what a world of unseen visions and heard silences, this insubstantial country of the mind! What ineffable essences, these touchless rememberings and unshowable reveries! And the privacy of it all!

Julian Jaynes, *The Origin of Consciousness in the Breakdown of the Bicameral Mind*

The poetic invocation above not only is apt as an introduction to Jaynes's thoughtful book, but applies equally well as a description of a fundamental problem of survey research: how do we find out what is in people's minds, and what does it mean in terms of its effects on human behavior? Any useful theory of questionnaire design must grapple with this question, which ultimately leads to psychology and personality theory.

Limitations of personality theory

Many questionnaires contain elements of psychology in the wording of specific questions and in the hypotheses underlying these questions. Such psychological approaches are used to try to explain *why* people may vary on a factor beyond what can be explained by demographics alone. For example, in an article on social attitudes toward the computer, Robert Lee makes the following statements based on personality theory:

People tend to react with awe and a sense of inferiority to this latter conception [of the computer as a relatively autonomous machine that can perform the functions of human thinking]. Individual variations

19

in the strength of these reactions to the computer are related to certain personality factors and life orientations that are highly pervasive in character.

To explore this issue, in addition to the usual demographic questions we also included in the questionnaire six potentially relevant psychosocial attitude scales: familiarity with the world of business, interest in current affairs, receptivity to the new and different, intolerance of uncertainties, and ambiguities, trustful optimism, and alienation.[1]

Another example of the prevalence of personality theory comes from a story in *The New York Times* of July 24, 1979, and the headline underscores the basic problem of applying personality theory in surveys: "Behavioral Scientists Argue Guilt's Role." The article gives quotes from eminent psychologists describing guilt as either "a destructive form of self-hate," or "a guardian of our goodness."

This type of approach as it applies to surveys means that the survey researcher, depending upon which view of guilt he holds, will design questions reflecting *his* perception of the meaning of guilt in human behavior. Or he will incorporate into his questionnaire a theory of guilt or violence or authoritarianism which he has picked up from a staff psychologist, leading psychology books, or other sources. Each psychological theory exemplifies the theorist's peculiar preoccupation. Ernest Becker's theory concentrates on man's society building and blind following of leaders as a denial of death. Rollo May emphasizes ennui and alienation as failures of love and will. Freud partially explains women's problems of identity in terms of penis envy. Abraham Maslow develops some theories of human behavior in terms of self-actualization.

It is very worthwhile to use surveys as a tool in developing personality theory or extending current knowledge of human personality. There is much psychological survey research designed for precisely these purposes, and it can be very valuable. However, random inclusion of personality theory in questionnaires not devoted *primarily* to development of theory raises many serious problems of questionnaire design, including excessive length, potential respondent abuse, and the costs involved in computer analysis which tries to make sense out of incomplete or incomprehensible questions dealing with respondent psychology.

1. Robert S. Lee, "Social Attitudes and the Computer Revolution," *Public Opinion Quarterly*, Spring 1970: 53, 56.

Although personality theory enriches our understanding of human behavior and tantalizes us with the complexity of human motivation, there is no single theory of personality which comes close to predicting all of human behavior. Because of this lack of a unified personality theory, questionnaires are often taken up with long series of items attempting to provide some theory to explain behavior, thus excessively lengthening the questionnaire while very often also failing to provide such a coherent theory. Listed below are typical statements which provide no predictive insight into the behavior of respondents or their attitudes. The items come from a study on perceptions of crime and the police on the part of the elderly.

> It bothers me when I have to swallow my pride and defer to the opinion of someone who has not had the experiences in life that I have had.
>
> Many times I feel that we might just as well make many of our decisions by flipping a coin.
>
> Most people don't realize the extent to which their lives are controlled by accidental happenings.
>
> Often I feel that I have little influence over the things that happen to me.
>
> Trusting to fate has never turned out as well for me as making a decision to take a definite course of action.

In fact, one of the most important findings to come out of this study resulted from *actual* behavior questions: the more time that people spent watching TV crime programs, the more likely they were to have unrealistic expectations of the police.

Throughout this book, I emphasize that the purpose of most surveys is to predict behavior. It has been our experience that personality theory rarely facilitates actual prediction of behavior when used in quantitative surveys.

Limitations of attitude theory

If current personality theories do not really help us predict human behavior, perhaps attitude theory can. Once again, however, we encounter serious problems, which include the volatility of attitudes, the effects of conflicting attitudes, and the lack of a clear relationship between attitude and behavior.

One indication of the volatility of attitudes is provided by the Gallup Poll. In the following example a national probability sample of the U.S. public was asked to state the most important problem facing the nation today. The responses were given over a period of months. (Only the top five answers are shown.)[2]

June 18, 1970	Campus unrest	27%
	Vietnam/Cambodia	22
	International problems	14
	Racial strife	13
	Cost of living	10
March 18, 1971	Vietnam	28%
	Economic problems	24
	Other international problems	12
	Crime, lawlessness	7
	Race relations	7
December 19, 1971	Economy	41%
	Vietnam	15
	Other international problems	8
	Drug abuse and use	8
	Racial problems	6
August 6, 1972	Vietnam	25%
	Cost of living	23
	Drug abuse and use	9
	International problems	5
	Crime, lawlessness	5
May 20, 1973	Cost of living	62%
	Crime, lawlessness	17
	Drug abuse and use	16
	Watergate, government corruption	16
	Pollution	9
January 31, 1974	Energy crisis	46%
	Cost of living	25
	Dissatisfaction with government	15
	Watergate/government corruption	7
	International problems	7

2. American Institute of Public Opinion, *The Gallup Poll*, Vol. III, 1959–1971 (New York: Random House, 1972); and American Institute of Public Opinion, *The Gallup Poll*, Vol. I, 1972–1975 (Wilmington, Del.: Scholarly Resources Inc., 1978).

May 2, 1974	Watergate/government	
	corruption	42%
	Energy crisis	33
	Nixon leadership	16
	Economy	13
	Breakdown in religious/	
	moral values	9
July 14, 1974	Cost of living	48%
	Mistrust of government	15
	Watergate/government	
	corruption	11
	Energy crisis	6
	Crime/lawlessness	4
September 12, 1974	High cost of living	77%
	Mistrust of government	7
	Watergate/government	
	corruption	3
	International problems	3
	Energy crisis	$<.5$
April 3, 1975	High cost of living	60%
	Unemployment	20
	Dissatisfaction with	
	government	7
	Energy crisis	7
	Moral decline/lack of	
	religion	7

Aside from the general problem of volatility of attitudes, these polls demonstrate that a significant variable affecting attitudes is saliency, in this case represented by the amount of time devoted to a topic in the daily press. Ironically, rather than demonstrating a relationship of attitudes affecting behavior, the above data seem to indicate that behavior affects attitudes: reading the daily newspaper determines how important a problem is perceived to be, and thus what attitude a person should take.

A clearer example of the tenuousness of any relationship between attitudes and behavior is that of the cigarette smoker who realizes that smoking is injurious to his health. He urges his children not to smoke. He admits that smoking is a dirty, expensive habit. His attitude toward smoking is distinctly negative, yet he keeps smoking. The whys of his smoking extend beyond his mere attitudes into personality theory. Does he smoke because of inner conflict, because it is self-fulfilling, or because he is fixated at the oral stage? None of these theories adequately predicts or even explains why a person who has a totally negative attitude toward smoking continues to smoke. They certainly do not predict if or when this person may quit smoking. All they indicate is that conflict in attitudes raises a key problem in predicting behavior using attitude questions in a survey.

Problems of priorities among attitudes

Even if attitudes were stable and related in some predictable way to behavior, we would still face the problem of measuring priority of attitudes among competing attitudes. The automobile driver maintains a very stable attitude toward his car, even though he belongs to the Sierra Club and writes letters to his congressman urging creation of new wilderness systems and supporting anti-pollution legislation. Yet he drives his car daily to work regardless of the escalating costs of gasoline and the pollution to the environment. If he were to give up his car, he would suffer withdrawal symptoms. Then OPEC raises prices and, more importantly, cuts supplies. Lines of cars snake for blocks around open gasoline stations. Our driver's attitude toward his car has not changed. He still prefers his car above all other means of transportation, but when faced with a choice between waiting in long gasoline lines or waiting at a bus stop, he finally capitulates and chooses the bus stop if that alternative exists. How can these priorities of attitude be measured when the situations that provoke activation of attitudes change so incessantly?

The relationship between attitudes and behavior

Milton Rokeach in his article, "Attitude Change and Behavioral Change," provides important insight into this problem of attitudes and behavior.[3] He identifies two sets of attitudes: those held toward a specific object, such as a man, a group, an institution,

3. Milton Rokeach, "Attitude Change and Behavioral Change," *Public Opinion Quarterly*, Winter 1966–1967: 529–550.

or an issue; and those held toward a situation, event, or activity. He states that people's attitudes can be activated by an object, by a situation, or by an object within a given situation. Public opinion polls measuring attitudes usually fail to make these distinctions or to analyze the data in terms of them.

A preferential response to an object cannot occur in a vacuum. It must necessarily be elicited within a context of some situation toward which a respondent will also have an attitude. As outlined by Rokeach, defining two sets of attitudes, which may or may not be independent of one another, leads to the following research problems:

1) How can we tell which set (the object set or the situation set) of attitudes is more important in predicting behavior at any given time?

2) How can we obtain a behavioral measure of a given attitude toward an object that is uncontaminated by interaction with a person's attitudes toward the situation?

3) When there is a change in behavior, how can we tell whether or not there has been a corresponding change in attitude?

4) If there has been a change in attitude, which attitude was changed—the attitude toward object or the attitude toward situation?

Rokeach defines an attitude as a relatively "enduring organization" of beliefs about an object or a situation predisposing one to respond in some preferential manner. However, an enduring organization of beliefs presupposes human awareness or consciousness of those beliefs, their sources, and their results. While personality theory as begun by Freud has grappled with the problems of the "unconscious" or the "subconscious" or repressed states of mind, research based on expressed attitudes usually evades or ignores this problem of consciousness or lack of consciousness, and rarely attempts to cope with problems of mere salience and its impact on so-called attitudes.

Consciousness, a definition

Salience can be defined as that thought, idea, or action which is uppermost in people's minds at any given time. The data quoted above on attitudes toward important problems facing the United

States present a classic example of mere salience masquerading as behavior prediction, or "attitude." The very act of interviewing a respondent makes an issue salient and creates respondent attitudes. Consciousness, on the other hand, goes much deeper than salience.

I depend upon the definition of consciousness outlined in great detail by Julian Jaynes in *The Origin of Consciousness in the Breakdown of the Bicameral Mind.*[4] Consciousness, to summarize Jaynes briefly, is a process whereby a person is able to arrange events and ideas together into new orders *within his head* as they may never actually have occurred either physically or in present reality. A person is able to excerpt pieces of knowledge or awareness and put them together into a story or narratization that makes these pieces compatible with each other. A person is able to see himself in his imagination doing various things, and then this person is able to make decisions on the basis of *imagined* outcomes before the outcomes actually have occurred in his real experience. A person is able to plot, to plan, and to visualize the outcomes of his future behavior.

At the conclusion of his development of a theory of what consciousness is and is not, Jaynes postulates, "If our reasonings have been correct, it is perfectly possible that there could have existed a race of men who spoke, judged, reasoned, solved problems, indeed did most of the things that we do, but who were not conscious at all."[5] While Jaynes does not apply that definition to twentieth century inhabitants of the United States, the responses obtained on thousands of surveys support the reverse conclusion: by and large, people may know what they have done, but they cannot explain why they have done it or what their behavior means. More importantly, from the point of view of predictive polling, most respondents cannot imaginatively put disparate pieces of information together into new patterns and then *imaginatively* visualize what their behavior would or would not be in response to this hypothetical information. This is why so-called measurement of attitudes by polls is ultimately so fruitless and puzzling to policymakers and so hazardous to people

4. Julian Jaynes, *The Origin of Consciousness in the Breakdown of the Bicameral Mind* (Boston: Houghton Mifflin, 1976), pp. 59–66.
    5. Ibid., p. 47.

whose future depends on the predictability of such polls.

All of our research experience indicates that on any given issue, few people have the ability to go through these *conscious* mental processes when suddenly asked, over the telephone and without prior notice, to expound on complex issues, such as those surrounding the Panama Canal treaties. In short, in a very deep sense, people cannot add. For example, at the height of the recent gasoline crunch, an acquaintance excitedly described a new electric vehicle, shaped like a bar stool, that had been developed. It could go 100 miles without needing its batteries recharged. Think how much gas would be saved! I asked her how the batteries would be charged. If they were charged through a standard electric outlet, that implied power provided by the local utility, and the power to run the local utility was provided by oil, and oil in an energy sense is equivalent to gas. Her face went slightly blank, and then she looked puzzled. "Well, I don't know about that," she said and ended the conversation.

We are all too familiar with the housewife who drives from store to store to pick up grocery "specials" to save a few dollars a week, and who does not consider the cost of gas and auto upkeep in calculating the price of the groceries. Or there is the person who drives his car to New York every day from South Jersey because it's cheaper and because he has not added the costs of gas, tolls, parking, insurance, upkeep, and wear and tear to his driving costs.

Corporate executives with supposedly superior intelligence often exhibit no greater consciousness. In recent conversations with the corporate marketing executive of a major bank, I discussed increasing market share at the rate of 1 to 2 percent per year, which at the end of five years could result in a 5 to 10 percent increase in market. This executive remarked that he had never really thought of it that way, and that I should make this point much more explicit in my report to his staff because they had not really thought of it that way either.

These types of calculations are rudimentary yet beyond most people's comprehension. More complex issues, which demand mental piecing together of information to form a total picture of an event or situation that has not even occurred, present problems even for well-educated, well-informed people.

Questionnaires and consciousness

If we analyze standard survey research questions in terms of need for consciousness, attitude toward object, and attitude toward situation, we can immediately see the shortcomings of this approach to determining human behavior.

Here is a typical attitude question from a survey conducted to predict human behavior:

> "If you knew that one of the commercial banks in this area was part of a bank holding company, would this fact make you feel more like doing business with them, make you feel less like doing business with them, or wouldn't it make much difference to you one way or the other?"

Analyzing this question from the point of view of respondent consciousness, we can discern that for a respondent to give a meaningful answer, one that is close to being true and predictive of subsequent behavior, he must first be able to project himself mentally into a particular picture. First, what is a bank holding company, and how does this affect him as a bank customer? Second, does a bank holding company mean a bank is bigger, has more regulations to follow, provides more services to customers, builds more banks, or what? If a bank holding company does all of these things, how does that affect him? Does it affect him positively or negatively? What is meant by positively or negatively? Assume that positive means more services at lower costs, and negative means higher charges for checking account usage.

If we analyze this question with regard to attitude toward object, it is apparent that the respondent must be conscious of his feelings or have feelings with regard to bank holding companies. That is, he must think they are either good or bad in order to answer this question meaningfully. To know this, he must have thought about bank holding companies. The respondent may think bank holding companies are good for banks but bad for corporations, or bad for small business owners, or bad for checking account customers. Or he may think that they lessen overall banking competition, or that they have a greater chance of making large, speculative loans and then going bankrupt. Or he may believe that bank holding companies provide more services to the average citizen, that they insure the average depositor against losing money in a bank failure and so forth.

If we analyze this question from the point of view of attitude toward situation, the respondent must be aware of the situation in his geographic area. Are all the banks in his area part of a holding company, and therefore the question is moot? If not, how convenient is the bank we are discussing? Is it more convenient to him than one that is not part of a holding company? If so, is convenience of more importance to the respondent than the fact that the bank is part of a holding company? Maybe he would feel more like doing business with the bank holding company if it also offered free checking accounts. If there is no drive-in window, he may never deal with a bank that is part of a holding company.

Obviously, the chance of *any* respondent's being sophisticated enough to know all of the above and then being able to weigh the pros and cons and give an intelligible, meaningful answer to an interviewer in the space of fifteen seconds is extremely remote. However, the respondent will give an answer anyway, and this answer will tell nothing about whether the corner bank's being part of a bank holding company will cause a decrease or an increase in customer volume, which is what the average bank client is most concerned about.

Such a question approach probes a respondent's "image" of a bank and gives expression to inchoate "impressions" of banks, which are then assumed to affect people's actual behavior toward banks or their actual support for restrictive legislation affecting banks, and so forth. This may be true, although I have seen little documentation that this in fact occurs when respondents are faced with a direct decision that bears immediately on their perceived self-interest. People may have a poor image of banks, but they still deal with them, and convenience (on the next corner) is a more important consideration to them than their subliminal image in determining actual behavior.

Another example of the problem of consciousness as it affects survey design concerns state government planning. A few years ago, New Jersey sponsored a social services needs survey. As a small part of this study, the state planning agency wanted to obtain some idea of levels of public support for social services needs within the state. A series of attitude questions was asked, one of which was:

"Do you think New Jersey is doing too much, too little, or about the right amount to help needy people?"

To give a meaningful answer to this (one that would reasonably predict how residents might vote on appropriations for social services needs), on the level of basic consciousness, the respondent would have to carry some mental picture of "needy" people. Are they people walking around without shoes, crippled people, alcoholic people, people without automobiles or without television sets, old people, people who are deaf and blind? Perhaps the respondent considered people like himself needy and that all people who could not afford to buy a steak for dinner that day were very needy. Then he would have to hold some idea of how many needy people there were in New Jersey. Were there 20, 20,000, or 200,000? If there were millions of needy people in New Jersey, maybe there was no way to do enough for all of them, and the issue was hopeless. If there were only two needy people, that wouldn't be a problem.

Then the respondent would have to view the issue in terms of government aid to the needy—the attitude toward object. Maybe this respondent thinks that need is a sign from God that a person is guilty of sin. Maybe this respondent thinks that needy people are needy because they are lazy and that, therefore, the government has no responsibility at all to help needy people. Perhaps he feels that the government should not provide aid but that private social service agencies should. Maybe he feels that the government should help but that the gradual increase in government services is getting out of hand and costing him too much in tax dollars.

Then we come to the attitude toward situation. Maybe our respondent favors government aid only to needy blacks, to needy women without husbands, to people who are physically crippled, or to people who are mentally retarded, but not to young people looking for jobs or old people who have families to look after them.

With all of these considerations, there is no possible way of really learning whether this person will in fact vote to support social service expenditures and absorb the resulting increase in taxes if we rely only on one or two general attitude questions on a poll.

Still other examples come from public policy on the national level. At the present time, considerable polling effort is aimed at developing public policy for lowering consumption of energy, whether electricity, automobile gasoline, or heating oil. All questions asked in this area of "would you be willing" face the same problems of consciousness and attitude outlined above. In terms of consciousness, now that the gasoline lines have shortened, people have again begun to increase their driving. The newspapers report a continued increase in the volume of traffic on major turnpikes and bridges and in tunnels, and parking lots in major cities once again are filled with cars each working day. The only consciousness that is now operating in people's minds is, "I don't have to wait in line for gas; therefore, there is enough gas for me to drive my car to work." Any further consciousness regarding continued consumption of gasoline increasing the rate of oil imports, thus increasing our balance of payments problems, and thus provoking higher prices from OPEC, which in turn increases our inflation rate, absolutely escapes most people. Yet they will say that inflation and the cost of living are the most important problems facing the United States today. In effect, their consciousness about the implications of their behavior does not extend beyond their ability to drive to and from work. Their attitude toward gasoline is, "If I can buy it easily, it's there." Their attitude toward the situation is, "If there are no lines at the gas station, I'll continue to drive my car regardless of the price of gasoline." However, a sudden cutoff in supplies would change this behavior immediately, as shown by recent events. The possibility that excess use of automobile gasoline in the summer may cut down available supplies of heating oil this winter does not occur to most people unless it is highly publicized by the media. Next winter they will berate the government for not providing enough heating oil.

The above examples deal only with questions where behavior would necessarily follow. I have not even attempted to discuss straight attitude questions in the area of public policy where no immediate or future behavior is even expected from respondents. These types of questions are even more likely to be plagued with huge discrepancies between level of consciousness, attitude toward object, and attitude toward situation. Nevertheless, presidents stake their political careers on responses to these types of global questions, while Congress makes policy, keeping similar polls in mind.

Summary of behavior-predicting components

Frustrated with the lack of predictability of purely attitudinal questions, and rather stunned by the huge gap between what people say and what they then do, I felt it necessary to re-evaluate the role of these types of questions within surveys and to find alternatives to them which could be used in predicting behavior. Consequently, attitude questions have become a minute part of surveys I design. They are replaced by questions that respondents can truthfully answer: questions concerning their environment, their knowledge, and their actual current behavior. To learn what is going on in people's minds and to relate it to potential behavior and present the alternative scenarios, I have incorporated Jaynes's concern about the existence of consciousness, Rokeach's categories of attitude toward object and attitude toward situation, and my own experience in conducting and analyzing data from surveys. The environment, knowledge, and actual behavior, as well as the level of consciousness in the respondent, all form the parameters of the *total* picture of the respondent's operating reality, and they comprise the *total* questionnaire. A questionnaire that incorporates only one or two of these concepts or parameters or deals only with respondent attitudes toward object without any concern for attitude toward situation or level of respondent consciousness can lead to policymaking disaster.

The environment: the surrounding situation or structures

I have rather narrowly defined Rokeach's attitude toward situation as the physical operating environment of a respondent. For example, while a respondent's attitude toward mass transit may be very favorable, the key determinant of whether he will use it or not is whether it exists in his environment. Similarly, while there may be many psychological reasons why old people will not go out at night, a major environmental factor is that old people commonly cannot see well at night. If I am old, I am also going to be more concerned about issues affecting Social Security payments and less concerned about education. If I am of child-bearing age, I am going to be more concerned about maternity benefits or contraception than if I am male or over sixty years old. In other words, the environment or physical determinants of behavior and attitude include such things as age, sex, health status, race, locale, and mobility—the physical aspects of his life over which the respondent has little control but which impinge on his ability to act or respond in specific ways regardless of his attitudes.

Respondent consciousness
By respondent consciousness, or awareness, I mean more than simply knowing that something exists in a subliminal way. I may be aware that it is hot outside without being really conscious of it. This mere level of awareness, such as an awareness that there is a Panama Canal, provides no insight into respondent behavior and is of little value in understanding these issues. By consciousness, I mean: does the respondent see or understand the *implications* of his answers to the questions? Can he add or fit pieces together to form a coherent picture? Where does he contradict himself, which indicates a lack of consciousness or lack of understanding of the issues? For example, if a respondent says he opposes abortion under *any* circumstances, and then proceeds to answer that he favors abortion to save the mother's life, favors abortion if the baby is a result of incest or rape, or favors abortion to prevent birth of a deformed child, we immediately discern a major discrepancy of consciousness on the part of the respondent. He does not see the implications or understand the meaning of "no abortions under *any* circumstances." He has given an unconscious or emotional response to the question.

Behavior
Documenting actual behavior serves several research functions. First, people are much better able to tell you what they *have* done compared with what they might do. Behavior sorts out the priorities among competing attitudes. Regardless of how important the environment is to a respondent according to his own testimony, his behavior—littering the roadsides, driving high-polluting automobiles, supporting industrial development over preservation of open spaces—indicates more surely what his priorities are, what his scale of values is. If there is a conflict of attitudes, the respondent favors one over the other by what he actually does

rather than what he says. The smoker smokes, regardless of what he says to you about his other attitudes.

Knowledge

Does the respondent really know what you are asking him about? Knowledge, or lack of knowledge, occurs on several different levels, all of which must be determined by the researcher before he can be sure his data are useful in predicting behavior. First, does the respondent know what the words themselves mean? Does he know what the word "inflation" means when you ask him, "How serious a problem is inflation?" Is his definition the same as yours? Does he say, "Inflation is higher meat prices," while you say, "Inflation is too much demand and too low productivity"? Are you both speaking from a common ground of understanding and common word definition? Does he know the United States imports oil? Does he know what the Panama Canal is? These may seem like ridiculous questions to you, the researcher, but if you ask respondents to define such facts or meanings on your surveys, you will soon learn that substantial numbers of people do not know the simple facts, and lack of this knowledge colors their attitudes and behavior and casts doubt on the usefulness of reporting such attitudes as a source of data for policy decisions.

☐ 4
Why do we need hypotheses?

The role of hypotheses

Several years ago, at the beginning of my survey research career with Opinion Research Corporation of Princeton, New Jersey, I learned the first principle underlying questionnaire design from Timothy D. Ellard, now senior vice-president of the company. Early one morning, clutching a cup of hot coffee, I meandered into his office to pick his brains and to pass a few minutes talking about malamutes, Norman Treigle (the outstanding singer at the New York City Opera), and Tim's daughter's progress with her tuba lessons. Tim had already drunk his coffee, and he was propped in an absolutely characteristic position: legs stretched out across the top of his desk, body leaning far back in his chair, gazing thoughtfully out his office windows into the gathering sunlight. I no longer recall how the conversation began, but I remember the most important principle Tim so casually dropped that early morning: the hypothesis is the basic building block of a well-written questionnaire. Developing the hypothesis provides the key ingredient to structure all subsequent parts of the project: the questionnaire, the sample, the coding, the tabulation forms, and the final report itself. If you develop your hypothesis and build your questionnaire around it, your data, as you collect them from the survey, exist to refute or support that hypothesis. "The most important work I do is to sit here in this chair, and stare out of the window or at the wall, and develop my hypotheses," Tim said, "and I look like I'm not working at all."

At the time, I had no conception of how pervasive hypotheses were to become in the development, conduct, and implementation of all my subsequent survey research projects. Because hypotheses are so crucial to survey research and frequently so completely ignored, I will spend considerable time discussing hypotheses and their importance in the following chapters.

There are several different categories or levels of hypotheses that the professional researcher must develop and answer if his project is to progress efficiently, if his project is to be implemented effectively, and if his project is actually to *solve a problem.*

The first category of hypotheses concerns the design and goals of the project itself—the research hypotheses. These include hypotheses regarding the nature of the problem to be solved, the nature of the respondents to be interviewed, the sample design, the topics to be included in the questionnaire, and the research methodology to be employed.

The second category of hypotheses includes what I shall call the professional hypotheses. These are hypotheses dealing with professional ethics in the conduct of surveys, such as problems of excessive questionnaire length and subsequent respondent abuse, respondent or client anonymity and its effect on respondent answers, and so forth.

The third category includes hypotheses about the client—the types of political problems the client has within his organization, his reasons for commissioning a survey research project, the reasons why the client treats you, the survey researcher, as he does. Formulation of these client-related hypotheses is absolutely essential if you are to be able to deal with the client effectively in the conduct and subsequent implementation of the project. These hypotheses can often determine whether your project will come in under budget or over budget, whether the client will be satisfied with the work, and whether the client will return to you for more work. Appropriate answers to these hypotheses determine whether you have in fact been responsive to the client's basic research problem.

Research hypotheses

A good questionnaire is a research tool used to support or refute hypotheses. It is a problem-solving instrument. Such a questionnaire is an advocate. It plays an active role and its goal is an action—ultimately to inform policy decisions. Seen from this perspective, a questionnaire becomes an actively probing instrument rather than a fishing expedition or a blank slate upon which data are imprinted. Hypotheses in research questionnaires provide the structure, purpose, and meaning for the overall research project. When firm hypotheses are held in mind during questionnaire design, they act as the winnowing agent, sorting out the useful from the nonuseful questions, eliminating the extraneous "itch-scratch" questions that meet the needs of curiosity but provide no actionable information. My most difficult problem with both new employees in training and clients is to convince them that we must do the prior thinking. We must formulate specific research goals and hypotheses, because we have no right to afflict unsuspecting respondents with a catch-all questionnaire approach, which consists simply of asking every question we can think of in the hope that perhaps some of them will prove fruitful in the subsequent data analysis.

An example of the importance of defining the correct problem for which the survey is to be used comes out of a trademark infringement suit brought by Charles Revson, Inc., against Max Factor & Company in 1977. The suit concerned alleged purchaser confusion between the Revlon fragrance, Ciara, and the Max Factor fragrance, Khará. Two surveys were conducted, one for Revlon and one for Max Factor. They differed in every major technical aspect, but their results were nearly identical. The survey conducted for Revlon consisted of a sample of 550 women interviewed in shopping centers in seven metropolitan areas geographically dispersed throughout the United States. Respondents were asked to pronounce various fragrance brand names, including Ciara and Khará, and then they were asked to rate them on a five-point scale of similarity: "identical," "very similar," "slightly similar," "not very similar," or "not at all similar." Using these question and sample techniques, the survey found that 56.6 percent of the entire sample responded that the names Ciara and Khará were "identical" or "very similar."

The study conducted for Max Factor used a probability sample of men and women. The respondents were shown the Ciara and Khará trademarks in logotype form rather than in typewritten form. The five-point scale of responses emphasized differences rather than similarities by using the expressions, "not different at all," "not very different," "slightly different," "very different" and "completely different." In this study 54.4 percent of respondents reported perceptions that the names Ciara and Khará were "not different at all" or "not very different."[1]

The court admitted that the two surveys corroborated each other's findings in spite of the technical differences between them. However, the court did not find that the surveys were germane to the real problem, which was *confusion* between the two products at the point of purchase. The court found that the study conducted for Revlon totally failed to simulate realistically the act of purchasing perfume, not only because the respondents were not shown the packaging of the respective products, but also because they were shielded from other purchasing cues, such as the scent, the price, the behavior of the clerks, samples, word of mouth from friends, advertising, sales promotion, and mailers. Furthermore, the court held that the surveys found no evidence concerning the relative importance of a product's name as a "cue" in the cologne and perfume purchasing transaction. The surveys failed to establish any relationship between the test of the relative similarity of the names and the concept of consumer confusion as to the source of products in the marketplace. They did not bridge the gap between a perceived similarity in the names Ciara and Khará and the ultimate issue of likelihood of confusion between the trademarks or the products.

Thus, the first basic design hypothesis is to help define the *real* research problem. Similarity of perfume names was not the real problem; confusion among consumers was. In a political study the real problem is how the candidate gets elected, not whether he is winning now. In banking the real problem is how the bank sells a financial service, not how many people are customers of the bank. In regulating sales of dread disease insurance policies,

---

1. United States District Court, Southern District of New York, *Charles Revson, Inc., Plaintiff, v. Max Factor & Co., Defendant*, Aug. 3, 1977.

the real issue is what the old people thought they were buying, not how many of them bought the policies. In a study of the relationship between the elderly and the police the real issue was not in what ways the police could behave better toward the elderly, but what the elderly thought of them and why. In other words, what is the client's *real* problem? Often the client has not articulated it himself, and helping the client define the problem becomes the first job of a good survey researcher.

Definition of the real problem then leads to appropriate design of the sample and appropriate design of the questionnaire. Defining the real problem leads to questionnaire content hypotheses in the areas of environment or structure, behavior, consciousness, and knowledge, as touched on above.

An important area of research hypotheses concerns the nature of the respondents. A major problem in the design of questionnaires and delineation of content areas occurs because questionnaires are constructed primarily by white, upper-class college graduates for administration to the general public or to important subgroups of the general public completely unlike the researchers themselves, such as black welfare mothers, Spanish-speaking populations, veterans, or the unemployed. For example, in studies of energy conservation behavior, different value systems of different population subgroups result in radically different attitudes and behavior regarding the conservation of energy. Upper-class, educated whites tend to see conservation as a moral cause, something one does for altruistic reasons, or, conversely, they believe that as long as they have the money, they can afford all the energy they want, and conservation be damned. Middle-income groups tend to conserve energy for direct financial reasons if they can see some significant economic reward for conservation. Poor and less educated respondents, on the other hand, who would presumably be most motivated by cost savings to conserve energy, often do not respond to this motivator. Waste of energy may indicate their feeling of power over their environment and their effort not to capitulate to the system, or it may indicate unconsciousness of the implications of energy savings on their economic well-being. Certainly, since they often live in rental housing, their efforts to conserve energy may benefit the landlord rather than themselves. If they are homeowners, they may not have enough income to make the initial investment necessary to reap the financial rewards of a more energy-efficient home.

All of these statements incorporate aspects of the reality parameters listed earlier: the respondent's level of consciousness, knowledge, and actual behavior, and the environmental structures that impinge on that behavior. Failure to retain a mental picture of *all* possible respondents and thus design a questionnaire that relates to all respondents (their language, their cultural patterns, their educational level, and so forth) results in a white, upper-class framework implicitly built into the questionnaire. This forces respondents into a pattern of answers which may not accurately reflect *their* sense of values, their specific situation, and their actual behavior. This is the anthropological aspect of questionnaire design, and it demands deep thought and empathy with the respondents.

Professional hypotheses

A problem endemic to the profession is that of excessive questionnaire length. On a purely pragmatic level, development of hypotheses is not only essential to provide quality research and accurate, actionable data, but it is also important to the survival and vitality of the polling industry.

Firms engaged in federal government evaluation surveys know how difficult it has become to get Office of Management and Budget (OMB) clearance on questionnaires, because OMB has become particularly concerned about spurious and intrusive questions, excessive length, and overall respondent abuse. Excessive length and spurious questions result directly from a lack of hypotheses embedded in the questionnaire to guide question formulation. The researcher, because he does not have any hypotheses to guide his line of inquiry, asks every question he can think of for fear he may leave something important out. He asks hundreds of questions in the hope that subsequent statistical analysis—"massaging the data"—will provide useful information to substitute for his initial lack of thought and mental exertion during the design phase of the questionnaire. Granted, all relevant hypotheses cannot be considered in advance of research. The research itself generates new hypotheses. However, inclusion of completely extraneous questions on the ground that "We might need them" or "This is something I'm just curious about, and

I'd like to write a paper about it some time later" constitutes respondent abuse.

Hypotheses prevent respondent abuse

Not only OMB but the responding public itself has become more and more conscious of this type of abuse. Response rates have fallen since the early days of polling. Personal interviews have become so difficult to obtain that telephone-interviewing facilities have burgeoned as a substitute for personal interviews. People have been lied to about polls which have really been ploys for sales calls. They have been told that a poll will last only "a little while" when in actuality it took an hour or more. Since all polling depends on the cooperation of the public, it is in the researcher's own interest to design a questionnaire that does not abuse respondents through excessive length or stupidly contrived, meaningless questions. As professionals, we have a professional trust in our relationship with respondents that goes beyond merely maintaining their anonymity to treating them as people whose time is every bit as valuable as ours. Certainly, it is our professional responsibility when dealing with clients to emphasize this aspect of our profession in intercepting the "itch-scratch" types of questions so dear to many clients (and researchers). Yes, it would be fun to know the answers to them, but how would the answers provide information on which the client could act? How do such questions refute or support our research hypotheses?

Every question, especially those concerning demographics, should refer back to the hypotheses being tested. Will the answer to this question refute or support the hypotheses? If not, why is it included? For example, knowing that total family income is provided by two wage earners rather than a single wage earner is often particularly valuable in financial marketing studies, but the actual occupation of the wage earners is useless in predicting specific bank selection behavior. If I know that one of the wage earners is a telephone installer instead of a policeman, how can that possibly tell me how he will respond to a 25¢ increase in checking account charges? Of all the surveys I have conducted

or been involved in, I have yet to see occupation accurately predict or correlate significantly with attitudinal or behavioral data
in the questionnaire. Although occupation is often used as an
indicator of socioeconomic status, I have found that other demographics (such as ownership and use of an American Express
credit card) act as more effective surrogates for occupation or
socioeconomic status, yet these questions concerning occupation,
which are tedious and time-consuming, are routinely included
in survey questionnaires.

Hypotheses guide the client relationship

Perhaps the most important question a researcher must ask is,
"Is the client on my side?" The answer to this question determines how well the researcher will be able to carry out the project.
If you can work well with the client, if you share the common
goal of getting the job done, the study will progress much more
easily and effectively. Establishing this rapport with the client
makes it possible to develop further client-related hypotheses
dealing with the political issues surrounding the study and the
problems of subsequent implementation of the findings of the
study within the client organization. These issues become important if you hope to maintain an ongoing relationship with the
client and work with him in the future, not just once but several
times. When a study is finished and then stashed away in the
"circular file," you can believe that you did not understand
your client and his needs, or that the client was not basically
sincere in the objectives he stated to you when commissioning
the study. In either case, his chances of seeking you out for
repeat business are remote. Perhaps equally important, your own
satisfaction and pride in a job well done are dissipated if not
destroyed, making your own career less enjoyable and less re-
warding. Such a study also wastes the valuable time of everyone
who works on it—the respondents themselves, the coders, data-
processing personnel, printers, and so forth—and contributes to
their disenchantment with their own work.

I wish to emphasize that meeting the client's needs, both
in terms of obtaining meaningful data and in terms of operating

effectively within the client's internal political climate, is not the same as fudging the data to make the client look good. Development of hypotheses that truly deal with the client's problems rather than hypotheses dealing with some "interesting" peripheral issues is the most important goal of preliminary client meetings. Although we have occasionally encountered a client attitude that conveyed the idea of selectively presenting data to bypass a problem rather than to solve it or reveal it, we have never found it to be in our interest, the client's interest, or the interest of business in our society as a whole to capitulate to these types of pressures.

□ 5
How to develop hypotheses

Use past research

Ideally, every research project should build upon previous work done in the field. I have mentioned the role of prior research in knowledge of types of savings account customers (they are not usually in a high income bracket if they also have high balances) and the role of transportation availability as a primary need of the elderly. So much research has been and is being done that it is a rare study that is designed and conducted completely from scratch without *any* prior research experience to guide the design. However, the weight of prior research experience can preclude extension of knowledge unless the researcher commits himself and his client to this goal. In many firms, because of budget and time constraints, the working proverb is, "Don't reinvent the wheel"; that is, don't rethink the problem. The effective researcher, however, derives satisfaction and delight from the research process itself and consequently works to extend his knowledge beyond that provided by existing research.

In a study of the relations between the elderly and the police, we hypothesized that television would be a good medium to use as a means of reaching the elderly with a public relations campaign, so questions on TV viewing habits were included. Analysis of the data indicated that the elderly's perception of the effectiveness of the police in solving crime was directly related to the number of hours they spent watching TV and to the number of crime programs they watched. The more television they watched and the more crime programs they watched, the more unrealistic were their expectations of actual police performance. These findings led us to hypothesize that television has just as serious an impact on perceptions of reality by adult subgroups as it does on children's perceptions. We have included questions on TV viewing habits in subsequent studies of social services needs and have found positive correlations in many instances with other key variables, such as joblessness, feelings of helplessness, and levels of dependence on the welfare system. This approach leads to a continual extension of knowledge, which is what research is all about.

Draw upon your own experience

One of the most fruitful sources of hypotheses is examination of your own experiences and feelings. As researchers we have one huge advantage compared to physical scientists—we are people and the objects of our research are people. This bond of common humanity guarantees that in many very fundamental respects we are similar to each other regardless of our socioeconomic status. Basic needs are common to all groups of people regardless of where they live or how they live, and these basic needs are the source of fruitful hypotheses in the development of research questionnaires.

By examination of your experiences and feelings, I mean a plumbing of your irrational responses, or your emotional responses, which are much less a product of culture and much more a product of your life as a human being. For example, some years ago a group of researchers was discussing how to respond to a government request for proposals to study employee and employer attitudes toward hiring former cancer patients. The consensus of this highly intellectual group of researchers was that this was a nonproblem. After all, who would be callous enough to hold a former illness against a potential employee? One of the researchers, however, blurted out, "If I were an employer, I would not hire a former cancer patient. Everyone I've ever known who had cancer eventually died, and I don't want to be around dying people, and I don't think the others in this office want to be around dying people either. Anyway, if I were an employer, I wouldn't hire them, because cancer treatments would increase the cost of my health insurance policies enormously." The other members of the group looked at the speaker and were shocked, but the emotional power and truth of her response were strong enough to convince the others of how they would approach the project, because it was a real emotional problem.

Studies of energy conservation and transportation consistently encounter the stumbling block of mass transit. Why won't people use it when it's available? My own experience as a poor student in San Francisco without an automobile gives me a partial clue. It was virtually impossible to carry enough groceries for two people onto a bus, off the bus, and the necessary five blocks to my apartment. Cars carry not only people, but things—groceries, shopping packages, house paint, ladders, lawn mowers to be repaired, golf clubs and bowling balls. Imagine carrying these things with you on the average city bus. It would be nearly impossible, especially if the bus were crowded.

The key ingredient here is *imagine what it would be like.* Put yourself in that other person's shoes. Imagination and empathy are two keys to a responsive questionnaire, and they can be cultivated by deliberately reaching out to meet and talk with people from different socioeconomic classes and different life experiences. Unfortunately, researchers tend to eat their lunches, drink their cocktails, and play tennis with people who are just like themselves. They become isolated from reality, or at least from the different realities of people who don't play tennis and who bring their lunches to work in a brown bag or a lunch kettle. For example, recently the newspapers reported that Bell System communications workers are bringing action against the company over the issue of "potty" breaks. Operators must still raise their hands to request permission to go to the bathroom, and permission can be withheld for as long as thirty minutes. How many survey researchers must raise their hands to request permission to go to the bathroom? Thousands of workers throughout the United States on production lines in manufacturing plants must ask permission before leaving their immediate place of work for any reason. These basic environmental differences profoundly affect people's expectations of what they are entitled to, what their obligations are, and what their psychological rewards are, leading to profoundly different attitudes and behavior. To write a questionnaire that has any meaning at all to these different groups of people demands that the researcher know and sympathize with their mode of life. It is critical for the researcher to imagine how he himself would feel and behave if he lived and worked in a similar life environment.

Talking with people who work at totally different types of jobs can be crucial to understanding the variables affecting behavior. I casually mentioned to my husband a proposed study for determining public favorability toward bond issues for public construction, particularly highway construction. My husband spends most of his workday traveling over New Jersey's highways. His response was, "I don't want any of my money spent on new highways, but if they don't fix up these damned potholes, I am going to lose my truck in one someday." So I wrote two questions on highway construction: one to determine support for money to repair *existing* highways, and one to determine support for money to build *new* highways. In fact, favorability toward repair of existing highways was very strong, while support for construction of new highways was very weak, but both responses could have been lost and the basic motivations totally misunderstood if only one question about overall highway construction had been asked. I would not have conceived of this distinction if I had not talked with someone who spends most of his working days driving, instead of pushing paper.

Besides these very personal methods of hypothesis development—examination of one's own feelings and personal contact with people from widely varied life-styles—three professional approaches to hypothesis development are commonly used by survey researchers:

1) Hypotheses obtained directly from the client.

2) Hypotheses obtained from past work in the field.

3) Hypotheses obtained from focus group interviews and individual, exploratory, in-depth interviews.

Hypothesis development with clients

After personal self-exploration, the second most important source of relevant hypotheses is the client. In the broadest sense, hypotheses obtained working with the client are those which not only guide the specific research, but also bear on successful completion of the project and subsequent implementation of the findings.

The client is directly connected with the problem, is most concerned about it, and has the most experience with the various issues. Furthermore, and very important to the study, the client operates within his own organization, which influences his decisions about the scope and nature of the research project. At the beginning of the project the researcher who will be designing the questionnaire should meet with the client and, making it perfectly clear what he is doing, conduct an exploratory in-depth interview to draw out all relevant hypotheses.

There are three purposes of this client interview. The first is to obtain all the hypotheses that the client himself is aware of. This will also give you important insight into how the client perceives his business, what his essential business goals are (for example, maximization of profit, development of high-quality products, innovation, corporate growth, or enhanced position of power within the organization itself). The second purpose is to insure that the client has not been blinded to some important hypotheses by his own closeness to the problem. You, as the outside researcher, may see these hypotheses which he has not. The third purpose is to determine what type of client you are dealing with and how he fits into his organization. You use this client meeting to formulate hypotheses about the client which will help you in your dealings with him to bring the study to effective completion and subsequent implementation if possible. Chief among these hypotheses is whether the person you are dealing with directly is the one who wields the power, or whether he is just a mouthpiece for someone higher up with whom you ultimately must deal, even if not directly.

The first purpose, obtaining all possible hypotheses known to the client, is the easiest to accomplish. However, often the client's hypotheses are the most obvious ones, and of course if he really knew everything, he would not have sought you out for help in the first place. Therefore, you must begin to go beyond these initial suggestions and probe the client's thinking as well as your own to identify further hypotheses for research. For example, whenever the client makes a flat statement about his market, the researcher should ask, "Why do you think that is true?" "Do you have any hard data to support that view?" Often you will find that the client is making a statement of fact which is really a statement of opinion or belief, unsupported by any sound data. Furthermore, clients often make statements about their problems in a vacuum, with little knowledge of the surrounding environment. For example, bank clients will make assumptions about the potential growth in their market without any hard data at hand on the population trends in their markets. Is the population increasing or decreasing? Is it a young population or an old population? Is it a stable population or a transient one? To be able to respond intelligently to this problem of an environmental vacuum, researchers must be widely read in a variety of fields, and I have found a basic knowledge of demography to be the most valuable tool in working with clients on either basic marketing problems or basic social problems. The rules of demographic changes in populations (birth rates, death rates, fertility rates, migration rates, and so forth) affect all areas of society, and the ability to explain and amplify the environment surrounding a client's problem through an understanding of demography can significantly enhance your ability to design a survey to solve that problem.

As a survey researcher, one of my most difficult problems has been to believe that I myself may see issues which the client, with all his experience and knowledge, may not have thought about. With my general education and nontechnical background, it is difficult for me to convince myself as well as the client that there are certain basic principles which apply to all types of problem solving regardless of the specific business he is in. Demographic principles are one example. Generalists often feel at a disadvantage before specialists, but the ability to see the large picture, a skill more often available to generalists, can be crucial to problem solving for any client who is too caught up in his immediate situation to see beyond his office door. This is the second purpose of the client interview.

To avoid feeling or appearing stupid in the interview, the researcher can gently probe with standard questions that keep the client talking and apply to any situation: "Why do you think that is so? Tell me more about your business so I am sure that I understand everything. Please explain to me what you mean when you say_____." The client's answers to these questions, in addition to distinguishing mere hunch from genuine knowledge, also let you know how deeply he has thought about his problems.

A second line of questioning which focuses client energy is, "If you knew the answer to that question, how would you use the data?" As mentioned earlier, and reiterated throughout this book, I believe the researcher has a professional obligation to force the client to clarify issues and restrict the problems to be investigated to *actionable* data gathering rather than mere curiosity. Money and time are at stake. Neither should be wasted by flaccid intellectualizing by either client or researcher.

You may feel exposed in this interview, and certainly you risk appearing uninformed if not downright stupid by asking some of these questions. More often than not, however, your client can give you an intelligent and valuable answer, and if not, these types of questions will provoke him to debate with you about possible new hypotheses. Remember, too, that this interview is a two-way communication effort; the task is not easy for the client either. He does not want to appear stupid about his own business, in which he has invested so much time and energy, and he may be reluctant to expose his own lack of knowledge. Part of the researcher's task is to create a climate in which the best possible job can be done. This mutual aim and good will enable you both to continue exploring and probing the issues.

The third purpose of this in-depth interview, raising hypotheses about the type of client with whom you are dealing, may present even greater diplomacy problems for you. How do you handle a client who doesn't want to hear what you have to say? How do you handle a client who won't tell you what you need to know to do a good job? How do you handle a client who fails to see the nature of the real problems facing him and insists on focusing on superficial issues? Failure to resolve these questions can result in a meaningless study or even abandonment of the project. If you cannot achieve rapport in the development of the hypotheses and research framework of the project, your chances of establishing a good working relationship with the client are slim.

Recently, a client who represents a major charitable organization came to our offices to discuss a study. His hypotheses revolved around the name of the organization: the name was dated, it was inappropriate to the current activities of the organization, and it was probably offensive to some segments of the population. Ostensibly, he was merely interested in a name test among members of the general public to confirm his opinions.

I began an in-depth interview with him. Why was he concerned? How would this data about the name of the organization affect his policy decisions? He responded that it was important to the effective implementation and conduct of their work, but as we talked further, his conversation constantly emphasized fund raising. The organization's contributions had been falling steadily, both in total number and in total dollar size. They had not been able to attract any new contributors, and their current contributors were aging. He attributed this decline in contributions to "inflation." He insisted that the organization was using the most up-to-date mailing techniques and that their approach to obtaining contributions was not the issue. Almost in passing, he mentioned that if they reached a large contributor, one who gave $20 or more, the contributor was "hit" with several requests for contributions during the succeeding months.

I thought of my own mailbox full of junk mail, and how I would feel if I'd just given a big contribution and was suddenly beseiged with additional requests for money. In fact this had recently happened to me, and it had made me mad. I suggested to the client that such an approach to his large donors may in fact "turn them off" and that it really was a form of negative feedback to the donors to be harassed this way as a reward for large donations. He rejected this hypothesis. In fact, he became more and more obdurate in his position and was completely unwilling to accept the idea that new fund raising organizations, particularly civil rights and environmental groups, had successfully attracted massive new constituencies which contributed much higher per capita donations than the old line charitable organizations. I suggested that perhaps the issue was indeed one of approach and type of appeal rather than a mere name change. As the conversation progressed, I saw very clearly that the client was unwilling to listen to my suggested hypotheses. Somehow these civil rights and environmental donors were different (which is probably true, but then we should ask why they are different and in what ways), and he rejected them as unattainable without trying to examine how similar techniques and approaches might be applied to his own fund raising problems.

Clearly, as a consultant I now faced a serious problem of my own. Should I backtrack and focus only on the issue as the client originally presented it, which would be responsive to his short-term need, but quite possibly unresponsive to his long-term need? Could I in some way persuade him to test the additional hypotheses I had raised, which would expand the nature of the original study as the client had proposed it? In this meeting I had not only been successful at developing new research hypotheses, but had learned so much about the client himself that I was in danger of abandoning the project unless some accommodation could be reached. It seemed highly unlikely that we would be able to work together given the client's very firm view of reality, which was diametrically opposed to my own perceptions and personal experience. However, by giving some ground on some issues while trying diplomatically to draw people from the client's advertising agency (who supported me) into the argument as moderators, an accommodation was reached, and the project continued.

When interviewing a client, or anyone for that matter, I use two listening techniques to identify client priorities and values. The first consists of listening for repetition of certain words. In the above example, although the client first talked about name change, as the interview progressed, he constantly repeated the words "fund raising." These two words, combined with "money," showed where his real problem or concern lay, even though he himself had said it was name change. In conversations with other clients the key repeating words may be "company politics," or "growth," or "profits," or "prestige."

The second technique consists of listening for silences, identifying what has *not* been said. Often the client will not mention something so key and so significant that its omission begins to look very suspect. Why is the obvious being avoided? This technique is more ticklish, but equally important. When this big hole begins to appear to the researcher, he had better bring it up or he could be in real trouble. If he ignores it, he is quite likely to fall into it.

We have an axiom in our company that says, if the client is truly interested in getting the job done, he will tell you *everything* you need to know to get the job done. With this basic approach to client relationships, this basic faith, there is no such thing as a really stupid question. If you find that the client evades your questions, or treats them (or you) as if they are stupid, or gives you an answer that does not seem genuine, or withholds key information (the silence), then you must conclude that either he does not want to get the job done, or you don't understand what job has to be done.

Several years ago I had luncheon with a potential client in a large New York bank, who said that he definitely wanted to conduct a major retail marketing study and that he very much wanted to work with my firm. During the luncheon, I was struck by how vague his specifications were and how uninterested he seemed in the project under discussion. He said that he wanted 1,000 interviews in the 5 boroughs that the bank served, and then he gazed out the windows and ogled the waitresses. I pressed him with questions. Did he have in mind some minimum income level below which we should not interview? He hadn't thought about it. I knew enough about his retail marketing area to realize that about 25 percent of it was lower income, at that time less than $5,000 household income (demographics again). If we were to interview among this group, our costs would go up dramatically, but we would not obtain any useful information about financial service usage for the bank since this group was a very low net user of such services. Did he want to include the Spanish-speaking subgroups? That would mean Spanish language questionnaires or Spanish language interviewers. No, he didn't think so. I became angry at his perfunctory responses. He would not tell me anything that I needed to do the job correctly. I had to force answers from him. I concluded from his lack of interest and his overall demeanor toward me that he did not want us to do the study, that he was only using us to obtain a "competitive" bid which would be much higher than that of his preferred, but secret, supplier. This hypothesis regarding the client was later borne out, when the study was awarded to a former employee of the bank with whom he was great friends and who had set up his own small consulting firm.

Thus, exploration of hypotheses regarding your client is essential if you do not wish to waste your time, and it is also essential if you want your study to be accepted and used within the organization. Frequently, we include some questions on a questionnaire which merely support the conventional wisdom held within the client organization. Or the client himself tells us that his boss needs to know something that confirms his pet hunch, and we'd better include it or he will not accept the study. By including these types of questions (but keeping them at an absolute minimum) and becoming familiar with the internal politics of the organization, we have a better chance of seeing the balance of the study accepted and implemented.

Focus group interviewing

A focus group is the best known and most visible means of hypothesis development. It can briefly be described as a group of individuals gathered into a room equipped with tape recorder, a one-way mirror for observation purposes, and possibly videotape if desired by the client. The group discussion is guided by a moderator, often using a topic outline. Focus groups consist of between six and twelve respondents as a rule, although the numbers can vary. They can last from one to three hours without boredom to respondents or moderator, depending on the inherent interest of the topic.

Before even recruiting for a focus group, the researcher should have developed preliminary hypotheses from his own experience and that of his client. He will need these hypotheses in mind to develop the topic guide for use in the discussion and to help him decide what types of people should be invited to the session.

In a study concerned with the location and building design of a bank to be established near a retirement community, I recruited elderly residents for three group discussions. Before going into the study, the client and I explored the following preliminary hypotheses:

1) The elderly will want a bank designed to look solid, dependable.

2) The elderly will want a bank designed with ramps instead of steps.

3) The elderly will want places where they can sit in the lobby.

All of these hypotheses were supported by the research, but two critical new hypotheses emerged from the focus groups: The elderly would like immediately accessible bathrooms, and they would need a bus running from the retirement community to the bank, since they did not have their own cars.

Moderation techniques

The moderator of the group will need hypotheses to help him decide how he should conduct the session. Should he interject himself or remain a silent observer? Should he handle the topic with kid gloves or plunge directly into it? Will he need a trained psychologist to run the session, or can he himself do it?

How a person moderates a focus group tends to be a matter of personal style, as well as what approach will most impress the client. Often, a trained psychologist is needed. Certainly, many topics are so sensitive and subjective that a psychologist's approach and technical skills can be invaluable. However, many topics do not need this level of effort. In fact, approaching them this way may be detrimental. You may look for something so deep that you miss the essential truth of the matter, which may be shallow but real nonetheless.

People within the research community argue about whether the moderator should sit quietly and say nothing—a nonobtrusive approach which creates tension within the group, which in turn supposedly provokes people into blurting out their innermost feelings—or whether the moderator should actively participate in the discussions to build greater intimacy among the participants by making him less of an observer. Regardless of which approach is used, moderation of focus groups demands the same sympathy, empathy, and alertness that are so essential to all phases of questionnaire design. The approach of the moderator will have to vary depending largely on what works best with a particular group of people. Some groups are voluble and engaged, others are aloof and silent. If you have a silent group and an equally silent moderator, not much hypothesis development will occur.

The sensitivity to be applied in moderating a focus group is nowhere more important than in deciding how sensitively the subject should be handled. For example, in focus groups conducted on a new type of toilet seat, the moderator, aware that this was a sensitive topic, treated it as though it were sensitive and did not directly mention toilet seats at the beginning of the focus groups. Consequently, his respondents became embarrassed at his embarrassment, and they covered their discomfort with bathroom humor and ribald jokes which did not really help cover the topic at hand, which was toilet seat design, color, and how often people would be willing to replace a seat. In this case, it probably would have been more effective for the moderator to state the purpose of the group discussion in order to get the embarrassment immediately out of the way and insure that all respondents knew the topic and could settle into the discussion comfortably. It can be argued that this very discomfort may produce important psychological hypotheses about people's most intimate feelings about bathrooms. This is certainly true, but these same deep emotional feelings may not come into play when deciding whether to purchase a blue or a white toilet seat.

Another example of sensitivity gone slightly awry occurred in focus groups dealing with pesticide and herbicide use. Farmers were being interviewed, and the moderator, no farmer himself, kept trying to ascertain what factors or aspects of a pesticide were most important to the farmers—the packaging, the weight, the cost, the mixing techniques, and so forth. Finally, one exasperated participant commented, "We want it to kill, damn it, to kill!"

Respondent selection
To be effective as a means of research hypothesis development, focus groups must include people who are relevant to the problem being explored. In a recent bank marketing study the client was concerned about different types of savings accounts, such as regular 5 percent passbook accounts combined with 6 percent accounts where the customer would split his savings (keeping part at the lower rate of interest so he could withdraw it readily and part at the higher rate where he would earn more interest but be subject to withdrawal restrictions). The primary criterion used for selection of respondents for these groups was that they have a high income, on the assumption that only people with substantial incomes are able to save money. When the group sessions were completed, they had not generated any new hypotheses of note, except that high-income people don't put their money into savings accounts to begin with, so they were not interested in the new product. These people put their money into stocks, bonds, and real estate, and they borrow because of the tax advantages. They do not keep significant amounts of cash lying around in low-

interest savings accounts. On the contrary, as past research has shown, the greatest users of bank savings accounts and those people with the highest balances are usually low-income or retired people with little education and little financial sophistication. Savings accounts are often the only avenues of investment open to them because of high balance requirements for treasury bills and other investments. Furthermore, these people are very conservative financially, and they want their money where they can see it and reach it easily. Focus groups comprised of relatively low-income but elderly respondents with higher savings assets would have been much more likely to produce hypotheses useful to the client in marketing savings products.

Selective nonresponse
While recruiting relevant respondents for focus groups is essential to effective hypothesis development, systematic refusals by certain types of respondents to participate in such groups may also lead to very fruitful hypotheses. When recruiting elderly respondents for the bank design study mentioned above, I had great difficulty obtaining enough respondents because people were refusing on the grounds that they could not get to the focus group session. Consequently, I arranged to chauffeur the respondents to the sessions. This lack of transportation, as mentioned earlier, emerged as a serious hypothesis to be considered in the location and design of a bank. If all people who could not attend because of transportation problems had been excluded from these sessions, this hypothesis might not have arisen. Once again, past research experience, particularly research on social services needs, has shown that lack of transportation is a serious issue affecting all aspects of the lives of the elderly.

Refusals to be interviewed also occurred at an alarming rate in an electrical connector study, and prompted the researcher in charge of the project to investigate why these people refused to participate in a group interview. It was a case not of "I don't want to," but of "the nature of the work and the type of firm in which I work bear no relationship to the issues you will be discussing in the group." To the client and the researcher, this came as a complete surprise, since they had not analyzed the problem in these particular terms. These refusals provided an important insight into how corporate structures (size, length of production run, number of engineers on payroll, and so forth) affect demand for industrial products, as well as insight into the most effective subsequent design and implementation of the ad campaign which was trying to reach certain types of engineers.

The two cases above illustrate the hazards of delegating all of the recruiting for group sessions to standard telephone interviewers, who have not been trained to be suspicious of types of refusals, and who have not been trained to pick up on offhand comments made by potential respondents when they refuse to participate. In particular, if respondents needed for a focus group are members of some special public, the researcher should plan to conduct some of the recruiting himself if he wishes to insure that systematic nonresponse will not jeopardize his study. While researchers are well acquainted with systematic nonresponse as a problem of mail interviewing techniques, similar nonresponse can have even more serious repercussions when it occurs in the hypothesis or design phase of a project.

In summary, hypothesis development is not some esoteric scientific exercise conducted by academicians. It usually takes no particular technical skill to develop hypotheses, but it does demand constant self-exploration, constant openness to new perceptions, and constant awareness of other people and their habits and life cycles. Everything is grist for the hypothesis mill—the newspapers, the magazines, casual conversations with your neighbors and colleagues. In fact, the chief prerequisite for hypothesis development is to have a garbage-can mind. That is, you need the type of head that collects every piece of apparently useless information for its own sake, because someday you will probably need it to formulate a study hypothesis. Hypotheses form the very spine of your daily work in questionnaire design. A hypothesis is like a Christmas tree, and all other research concerns of sample design, question wording, and analytical techniques become ornaments hanging from it. Without the tree itself, these ornaments cease to have any meaning or purpose. You will need hypotheses to understand the nature of the problem to be researched, to guide you in determination of the methodology to be used, to understand the nature of the respondents to be interviewed, and to understand and deal with the client who will ultimately accept or reject your study.

□ 6
Questionnaire structure and respondent meaning

The problem of attitudes

In Chapter Three I discussed the theoretical research problems inherent in a questionnaire which consists almost solely of attitude questions, or a study of attitudes. From a research point of view, studying attitudes means trying to distinguish between attitudes toward an object, attitudes toward a situation, and attitudes toward a specific object within a changing situation. Furthermore, any study of attitudes is complicated by the problem of respondent consciousness and respondent knowledge. Does the respondent understand what he is telling us? Does he see the implications of his attitudes? Does he even know what he is talking about factually?

Beyond these problems, perhaps the central issue is, how do we cope with volatility of attitudes, and how is volatility related to salience? How do we measure conflicts in attitudes and problems of priorities of attitudes? Most importantly, how do we establish a firm relationship between attitudes and specific behaviors? How accurately do attitudes *predict* future behavior?

My answer to the above questions is that at this time, in most cases, we cannot determine future behavior from a study of present attitudes. There is no way that we can separate out attitudes toward objects, toward situations, toward objects within situations using questionnaire techniques. Indeed, in most cases, we cannot truly identify a solid link between attitudes and subsequent behavior. The relationship between what people tell you they will do and what they in fact will do cannot be depended upon.

Nonetheless, we can impute or identify the solidity and significance of attitudes if we wish, but not by asking attitude questions. We can begin to predict behavior, but not by asking attitude questions or hypothetical behavior questions. Instead, we must concentrate on asking questions in the following topic areas:

1) Determination of levels of respondent consciousness.

2) Delineation of the structures or environments affecting behavior.

3) Determination of levels of respondent knowledge, both factual and computational.

4) Determination of present respondent behavior in specific situations.

Using these research tools, the researcher can approach the problem of attitudes as an analytical problem grounded in facts lying *outside* the respondent's invisible, unreachable, and unfathomable feelings or impulses. If necessary or desirable, he can, through analysis, impute specific attitudes to people, but whether or not he chooses to make this leap, he has at hand solidly grounded data reflecting the visible and apprehendable world from which to make policy decisions and predictions of future human behavior. The researcher no longer has to produce some vague or hypothetical proof of a relationship between attitude and behavior. He has learned what the respondent knows, what environment the respondent lives in, and what the respondent actually does. With this knowledge, the researcher can make better predictions of behavior than is possible through only a study of attitudes.

What do my answers mean?

When examining texts on survey methodology and approach, the reader becomes aware of a very strange omission, one of those silences that is so crucial. In all this discussion of research methodology, the authors emphasize problems of *bias*, which is defined as question wording that produces a favored answer or makes one response more likely than another, regardless of the respondent's real feelings. Then we encounter problems of *reli-*

ability. Evidence is considered reliable to the extent that similar findings would be obtained if the question were asked repeatedly of the same respondent over a period of time. And we encounter the issue of *validity*. Does the question actually measure the concept which is being investigated?

But nowhere do we encounter the problem of *meaningfulness*. Are the data meaningful? Data can be reliable, unbiased, and valid, and still not be meaningful, still not tell us what the respondent really feels, believes, or is likely to do. Answers can be meaningless, and they can be meaningless for several reasons.

First, the respondent can simply lie. He can lie to protect his real feelings, or he can lie because he does not want to appear stupid to the interviewer.

Second, a respondent may not give a meaningful answer because the questions as they were phrased and presented to him did not allow him to tell what he really thought, felt, or was likely to do.

Third, the respondent may not really know what he feels or thinks about the issue posed in the question. This is a salience problem and a consciousness problem. Or he may attempt to answer one question after another truthfully without realizing the inconsistencies or implications of his answers.

Fourth, the respondent can be giving us meaningful answers, but we may misunderstand what he is telling us because it is only a piece of a total picture. We may have failed to explore all relevant factors and features of the entire issue.

Fifth, a respondent can tell us how he feels or what he believes, but his answers will not be meaningful if his current attitudes and beliefs are derived from a basic lack of knowledge about the issues under discussion. More knowledge would change his basic attitudes.

Finally, we as researchers can be misled by respondent answers because we impute meaningfulness to them when in fact the answers may have no importance or salience to the respondent whatsoever.

In spite of all the possibilities of meaningless answers described above, the respondent will still answer questions, and those questions may be unbiased, valid, and reliable. Yet the answers to those questions will give us meaningless and even misleading information.

The client is paying for answers to his question, "What should

I do?" To answer this question, we must be able to determine the predictiveness of our data. How can we assess the meaningfulness of our answers? How can we know what we have when we have a lot of answered questions?

At this point, questionnaire design and data analysis merge. We must analyze our answers, but unless the questionnaire itself has been constructed with the built-in tools for this analysis to distinguish meaningless from meaningful answers, we cannot analyze the data and know what our results stand for. The remainder of this book describes ways of building analytical tools into the construction of the questionnaire in order to determine with greater accuracy actual respondent *meaning*, and I define one major aspect of meaning as predictiveness of actual behavior.

Constructing the questionnaire

Thus far, I have talked about what the survey researcher must do before he begins to write a questionnaire. Now comes the actual construction of the questionnaire. In the next chapters I will emphasize several basic concepts which clarify respondent answers and provide tools for analysis of these answers. These concepts are:

1) Determining levels of respondent *consciousness*.

2) Determining the influence of *structures* on attitudes and behavior.

3) Determining how *knowledge* affects respondent behavior and respondent answers.

4) Determining the importance of past *behavior* as a predictor of future behavior.

5) Defining the inherent multidimensionality of a problem.

Notice that there is nothing here about attitudes. Determining levels of consciousness helps identify whether people are *aware* of what they are saying or doing. We assume that policymakers would prefer to be guided by respondents who know what they are doing and saying, and whose responses are thus reasonably predictive of their future behavior, since respondents who are totally unconscious of the meaning or implications of what they currently say and do may exhibit more volatile and unpredictable behavior. Lack of consciousness is often indicated by answers that are inconsistent, not based in objective reality, purely emotional, ignorant, or misleading. If our data reflect a low level of respondent consciousness, no amount of fancy statistical analysis or data massaging will provide us with genuine guides to predicting behavior. Therefore, we have as much obligation to measure variations in level of respondent consciousness as we do to measure sampling variations and their impact on the reliability of our data.

Determining the influence of structures helps the researcher understand the context of respondent answers and the influences conditioning those answers. If respondents are unconscious, they are more likely to be heavily influenced by their environment. They are reactive rather than active. Determining structures places limits and boundaries on respondent answers. Many answers to questions can only be understood in a total respondent context. Without this context, answers may appear illogical, irrelevant, contradictory, or self-defeating. Without a thorough knowledge of the respondent's environment, the researcher can overestimate or underestimate the importance of some answers he receives.

Determining respondent knowledge and behavior are both methods used to learn the salience *to the respondent* of his own answers. Clients and researchers suffer from the occupational hazard of believing the problem they are surveying is vital and of huge significance to the public they are interviewing. In fact, this is rarely the case. Only by determining the salience of the issue to the respondent himself can we gain the necessary perspective on the problem to make sound recommendations to the client. Knowledge and behavior also indicate respondent priorities and values, help define sensitive topics, and deflate the prevalence of socially acceptable answers.

Problems which are inherently multidimensional pose special research problems which draw together questionnaire design and data analysis to identify complex ideas, such as levels of need and perceived importance of a topic versus perceived differences.

Thus, a suitable technique is of primary importance for determining respondent priorities and for defining sensitive topics and issues. This technique is based upon using respondent testimony that is founded in actual behavior and actual knowledge rather than attitudes. All of the concepts listed above must be built into the questionnaire simultaneously with the hypotheses in an attempt to answer the question every decent researcher must ask himself: "What do my answers mean? How much credibility do they really have?" In other words, the researcher must design the questionnaire not only to obtain answers to questions, but as a means of distinguishing between meaningful and meaningless answers.

□ 7
The problem of consciousness

Determining respondent consciousness

The basic hypothesis underlying most survey research is that respondents know what they are saying and are conscious of the meaning and implications of their answers. In fact, people are assumed to be conscious in the conduct of most aspects of their lives. Although psychology has given great credence to the ideas of the "unconscious" and subconscious behavior, generally these are regarded as aberrant states. The major departure of this book, therefore, lies in the belief that people—twentieth century people—are essentially unconscious, using Julian Jaynes's definition of consciousness. Only on this basis have we been able to account for many of the discrepancies that continually occur in respondent testimony on public opinion surveys. Only on this basis can we account for the huge gap between what people say and what they do. Since our most important research hypothesis is that most people are unconscious most of the time, according to Jaynes's definition, the major problem in the design of questionnaires becomes that of determining levels of consciousness in order to measure the meaningfulness of respondent answers. In surveys we now believe there is a problem of sampling error, which has been defined and is generally easily solved, and a problem of respondent error, which has not been defined, is not easily solved, but accounts for the major error in applying survey techniques to problem solving.

Thus, the first concept or method used to distinguish between meaningful and meaningless answers to survey questions concerns this uncharted realm of consciousness. There are two research factors involved in the problem of respondent consciousness:

1) Determining whether the respondent is conscious.

2) Determining for respondents who appear to be giving unconscious answers whether there is a framework, which we have not correctly identified, within which the respondent is giving conscious, meaningful answers.

Thus, we need to design a questionnaire which will determine whether each individual respondent is conscious or unconscious, or whether *we* have failed to understand the meaning and framework of a respondent's conscious statements. The answers received during an interview may appear to be meaningless or illogical unless we have designed some tools into the questionnaire which begin to tell us the source of the lack of logic.

The factors involved in developing a questionnaire which will illuminate the respondent's level of consciousness and his framework for answers include the following:

1) Does the respondent *know* what he feels or believes, or is he simply answering the questions? Even if he knows what he believes, upon what experience are these beliefs based?

2) Does the respondent foresee the implications inherent in what he says, and is he consistent in his answers over a series of related questions that probe different aspects of the same problem? Does he see the *whole* problem or only a series of unrelated pieces?

3) If the respondent is inconsistent in his answers over a series of questions, does this inconsistency result from unconsciousness on his part, or does it result from aspects of the problem or of the framework of the problem that are important to the respondent but that the researcher has not yet exposed or obtained from the respondent?

Does the respondent know what he feels or believes?

As a rule, people have not thought about and do not know their feelings about most issues that have not directly affected them. The Panama Canal issue, described earlier in this book, is one such issue for most people. Indeed, we have found that only on some specific, highly publicized, personal issues, such as abortion, do people know what they believe. They have thought about it, puzzled over it, and have arrived at some fairly definite and grounded opinions on the issue. The Vietnam War was another example of such an issue, although one in which opinions did significantly change over time, especially as more and more people in the country were directly affected by the war. These types of national issues have in common that they deeply and *personally* affect people.

In 1978, 32 percent of the general public said that they personally had known someone who had had an abortion. Among people between the ages of eighteen and twenty-nine, 50 percent said they had known someone personally who had had an abortion. Among those who were sixty or over, only 7 percent said that they had known anyone personally who had had an abortion.[1] These figures help explain the greater support for legal abortions to be found among the younger age groups. Direct experience has led to greater consciousness and greater perceived need. As the Vietnam War expanded, affecting more and more families personally, a similar change in perspective occurred, until finally a majority of the U.S. public swung from support of the war to opposition to it.

Thus, the first rule of survey research is to attempt to determine what the respondent feels about an issue and how deeply he feels about it. However, you cannot do that simply by asking the respondent, "How do you feel about such and such?" and then, "How deeply do you feel about it?" One way for the re-

1. Michael Rappeport and Patricia Labaw, "Abortion as a National Issue," prepared for the Planned Parenthood Federation of America, Inc., 1979.

searcher to deal with this problem of gauging the impact of an issue or problem on respondent consciousness is to determine how *close* to the issue the respondent is, and closeness for survey purposes is almost equivalent to firsthand (or secondhand, but fairly direct) personal *experience.* A person who has fought in Vietnam will probably know his feelings about that issue more thoroughly than a person who only had a friend in the war but did not actually fight. The second person will be more likely to know his feelings on the issue than a person who has never been in the war and does not know anyone personally who was fighting in it. Similarly, a person who has actually had an abortion will probably know her feelings more clearly on that issue than someone who has not had an abortion. However, someone who has not had an abortion but who knows a friend who has had one will probably know her feelings better on that issue than someone who has not had an abortion and does not know of anyone who has had one. I have found that feelings based on experience are much more stable than either feelings based on salience as a result of media exposure or feelings based simply on habit not related to any direct personal experience. In the area of sex education, a person with children receiving sex education in the schools is more likely to have thought deeply about the issue than a person whose children are grown and are no longer in the public school system.

Examples of experience-related questions to be included on surveys are:

"Have you personally ever had an abortion?"

"Has your girlfriend or wife ever had an abortion?"

"Have you ever used an automatic teller machine?"

"How often do you usually attend church or temple services?" (religious or moral commitment)

"I am going to read to you a series of things that people can do to make their opinions known. Please tell me whether you have *ever* done it. Have you done it within the past two years?" (political commitment)

1) Written a letter to your congressman or senator.

2) Voted in a *primary* election.

3) Voted in any election.

4) Passed out literature or worked on a political campaign.

5) Walked in a protest march or participated in an organized protest demonstration.

6) Belonged to or contributed money to a special interest organization, such as one supporting civil rights, the environment, or birth control.

"Have you ever called the police for any of these reasons in the past?

Tell me which of these things have happened to you personally during the past year." (attitudes toward and experience of crime)

1) Been beaten up at home.

2) Been robbed of money or other property when you were at home.

3) Had property stolen from your home while you were away.

4) Been bothered by prowlers.

5) Been vandalized or had property destroyed at home.

6) Been harassed or taunted by teenagers while at home.

These experience-related questions can then be used as a scale to analyze evaluation questions, such as favorability toward abortion, favorability toward the police, favorability toward the political system. For example, a person who has been beaten up and robbed is more likely to have thought about the role of the police and to have a *conscious* opinion of the role of the police or of the problem of crime in his area than a person who has never had firsthand experience with either crime or the police.

Is the respondent giving you a coherent picture?

One of the best ways of determining whether the respondent is conscious of his beliefs and their meaning is to ask a series of questions which will expose any logical inconsistencies in these beliefs. We have found that a logical progression of answers from a respondent indicates that the respondent has *thought* about a problem, rather than simply imbibed beliefs about it from his environment. Thus, a positive answer to the first question should logically be followed by a negative answer to the second, and so forth, if the respondent understands the meaning of the questions and the meaning and implications of his own beliefs. Random beliefs do not have direction, and behavior based on random beliefs is also likely to be random rather than directional. Part of the subsequent data analysis is to examine answers for direction, for logical progression or inconsistencies in progression which indicate lack of consciousness.

The following series of questions dealing with abortion was designed specifically to pinpoint logical inconsistencies and to follow them up for greater insight into the respondent's level of consciousness:

1) "What types of people do you think most need abortions?"

2) "When would you favor legal abortion?"

3) "If you favor abortion to save the life of the mother, why do you regard the life of the fetus as less important than the life of the mother?"

Some people answered as follows:

1) "Only unwed teenagers need abortions."

2) "I oppose abortion under *any* circumstances."

3) "I favor abortion to save the life of the mother."

4) "The mother should be saved rather than the fetus, because mothers are needed for other family responsibilities (they already have children, a husband, etc.)."

Note the importance of the *progression* and *order* of these questions. The answers show a completely inconsistent, illogical position, but reveal that the respondent was answering random questions based on random feelings rather than a coherent picture of the problem of abortion. The respondent is giving attitudes about teenagers, about killing, and about the importance of mothers. He is not giving a coherent picture of his feelings about the issue of abortion, because he has no coherent feelings about the entire issue, only about isolated facets of it. If public policy were to be made on the basis of the above answers, abortions

would be made available only to married women because only
teenagers need abortions.

Note also the importance of not accepting the first answer to
a question at face value. People will say that they oppose abortion
under *any* circumstances and then go on to say they favor it to
save the life of the mother, in cases where the baby will be retarded,
and in cases of rape.

Answers are typically inconsistent and unconscious in the
area of voting preferences:

1) "I vote for the man, not the party."

2) "What are the characteristics of the man you vote for?"
Answer: "Honesty."

3) "How do you define honesty?" Answer: "An honest man
is one who votes on my side of the issues."

4) "How do you know he votes on your side of the issues?"
Answer: "Because he is a Democrat."

Subsequent analysis of voting behavior shows without doubt
that although this voter says he votes for the man, in fact he votes
for the party. Experience shows that whether a person has voted
Democrat or Republican in past elections is a much better predictor of future voting behavior than anything he may say about
a specific candidate. In this case, the respondent is unconscious of
his reasons for his own behavior.

Another example of unconscious answers occurred in a study
of people with motor vehicle driving violations. The purpose of
the study was to determine the effects on traffic violators of
educational campaigns to change driving habits. When asked
whether their emotional state affected their driving at all, respondents would reply that their emotions had very little effect on
their driving habits. Then, when asked to describe the circumstances surrounding their last traffic violation, respondents typically replied, "I was mad at my girlfriend," or "I had a quarrel with
my wife," or "We had a family quarrel," or "I was angry with my
boss." Yet emotions did not affect their driving, they said.

These respondents are unconscious in three important ways.
The first consists of an inability to see a total picture and respond to it rather than to isolated parts. This is a very common
phenomenon. The second way in which people are unconscious

concerns the reasons underlying actual behavior. People often do not know or understand why they do things. They just do them. A third form of lack of consciousness consists of the inability to visualize the results of an action. This is part of the basic inability to see a *total* picture rather than isolated parts. A perfect example of this type of lack of consciousness arises when people are asked about taxes and government programs. People consistently answer that they favor increases in funding for education, national health insurance, Social Security for the elderly, and unemployment programs. Yet when asked to support these programs with tax dollars, they veto such an approach under the guise that increased services could be provided without increased taxes if only the government were more "efficient." When you pursue this idea of efficiency, you learn that, yes, people recognize that their own companies are inefficient, that inefficiency occurs with increases in the size of organizations, that the government is a huge bureaucracy, and that bureaucracies are usually inefficient. Another example occurs when people say that they oppose nuclear power plants, oppose loosening air pollution controls to allow more fossil fuel power plants to be built, and then insist that the utilities are not doing enough to insure that there is adequate electricity available for the future.

All of these respondents are unconscious. They do not see the contradictions in their answers. They do not add or connect isolated pieces of information into a coherent picture. As a consequence, we cannot be sure of what their actual behavior would be under any circumstances. We cannot predict their probable behavior with any degree of certainty, because they do not know what they think, why they do things, or what they would do, whatever they may tell us on a questionnaire. In spite of all this, the answer to any one question would fulfill the requirements of being valid, reliable, and unbiased. However, we would not know the meaning of the answer. We would not have any picture of the respondent's operating reality, which could at best be described as unconscious and confused. We are dealing with a respondent who is giving us a purely emotional reaction to specific words and phrases in questions. This is very important to know before we recommend specific courses of action to clients. The meaning of these data lies not in what respondents said per se, but in the pattern of their responses, the inconsistencies and non sequiturs in their answers.

Logical inconsistencies as a reflection of a complex respondent framework

While logical inconsistencies appearing over a series of questions can indicate unconsciousness in the respondent, they can also indicate consciousness of a very complex framework surrounding his answer. (It is a standing joke in the survey research business that an intelligent, thoughtful, detailed answer to a simple question is classified as "other" and obliterated.) It then becomes important for the researcher to identify this framework in order to understand the meaning of the respondent's apparently inconsistent answers.

In my preliminary conversations with people during the hypothesis formation stage of the abortion study, people would respond, "Yes, abortion is killing," "I don't condone killing," "I favor abortion." This answer series presents a classic example of logical inconsistency that plagues any polling dealing with this sensitive topic. In this case, however, the inconsistency arises because of the definition of the words "life" and "killing."

I began my attempts to understand these inconsistencies by questioning myself (self-examination) and others as to the meaning of the words "killing," "life," and "death." These words appear to be unambiguous, but in fact, when discussing abortion issues, people use these words ambiguously and respond to them ambiguously. If people oppose abortion on the grounds that it is killing, how do they justify killing the fetus instead of allowing the woman to die? Perhaps there are different definitions of "killing" depending upon the nature of the object being killed, and perhaps there are different definitions of "living" depending on the nature of the object that is alive.

Answers that pinpointed the semantic problem were:

1) "Abortion is killing."

2) "I oppose killing."

3) "I favor abortion, even though it is killing, because the mother is already alive."

In other words, people were making an important distinction between stages of life: developed life in the mother and undeveloped life in the fetus. Furthermore, they were making a value judgment about the relative quality and merits of each type of life. While respondents would not absolutely deny the life rights of the fetus, if a choice were to be made between the life of the mother and the life of the fetus, the mother's life should be saved because she is "more alive."

Textbooks tend to emphasize that respondents, when exposed to a series of questions, will deliberately try to answer consistently, whether they mean it or not. My experience indicates that a respondent's efforts to be consistent are often not the problem. In fact, a respondent often responds to issues illogically, not because he is lying, but because either he is simply unaware of what he has said and what it means, or the researcher has not explored the respondent's internal framework thoroughly enough to understand the logical inconsistencies. The researcher has an obligation to resolve this research problem. When subsequent data analysis shows that 24 percent of those people who said they would not favor abortion under *any* circumstances also go on to say (in a different part of the same questionnaire) that they would support abortion to save the life of the mother, and abortion to prevent birth of retarded children, and abortion in the case of rape or incest, you as the researcher are confronted with an analytical problem which you had better be prepared to discuss and understand. Designing a questionnaire in which identification of the problem of consciousness is built into question sequence is one way of beginning to cope with this research problem.

Too often these types of research inconsistencies are deliberately left out of the analysis and simply ignored. All respondents are treated as equal, and all answers are treated as equally meaningful. It is much easier for all concerned to say that respondents are conscious and rational and that their testimony can be accepted at face value than to admit that we don't know what we are doing or how to explain these inconsistencies.

The following are basic questionnaire techniques that can be used to identify problems of respondent consciousness:

1) Gauge the depth of understanding of an issue or problem by determining the *nearness* of a respondent to it through actual experience or levels of experience. Those people who have actual experience are more likely to be conscious of their answers, because the experience has forced them to think more about the problem or feel more deeply about it.

2) Determine the respondent's ability to see an entire picture rather than random parts by asking a series of questions outlining the different facets of the issue, and then check answers to see that the respondent answered all the different questions logically and consistently.

3) Determine the respondent's framework within which he is answering questions by asking a series of questions to outline the framework, and by asking open-ended questions which allow the respondent to tell you more of what is inside his own head, and allow the respondent to explain to you what he means by his answers. (The topic of open-ended questions is discussed at greater length in Chapter Thirteen.)

4) Determine the respondent's ability to understand his own behavior by concentrating on the respondent's actual behavior: what he did, when he did it, what the circumstances surrounding his behavior were. Analyze his answers in terms of actual behavior. Do his stated reasons for his behavior correspond to his actual behavior, or do they seem unrelated?

□ 8
Structures and environment

The influence of structures

The second concept around which questionnaires should be designed as a means of identifying "what you've got" in a respondent's answer pattern is to obtain and analyze the data in terms of the structures or environment surrounding the respondent and influencing his answer. Analyzing structures roots the respondent's answers in reality, takes the answers out of the realm of fancy, impulse, or pure attitude lacking any visible foundation.

I have placed this section on structures after the section on consciousness, because I believe that until a man is conscious, he is manipulated, a pawn at the mercy of his environment. Until a person understands the world around him, he will react rather than act. As soon as a person becomes conscious, he can and will act, rather than wait to be acted upon. Scientists and social scientists argue about the relationship between structures (the environment) and mankind, between the environment and man's attitudes. William Peterson, in his book *Population*,[1] begins his discussion of the study of population by explaining that while man is a biological being, suffering the immutable facts of birth and death like any other animal, man more than any other being is not passive. When his environment changes, he changes. More

1. William Peterson, *Population* (New York: Macmillan, 1975.)

than that, man shapes his environment to suit his needs. Psychologists, anthropologists, and other social scientists are split on the relationship between man as an animal and man as a member of culture, between man the manipulated and man the manipulator.

However, surveys consistently indicate that until we have definitely identified that our respondent is conscious, and thus capable of understanding and acting independently of his environment, at least to the extent possible, we must assume that the environment is acting upon him. This is a research decision that we have consciously made, although it may be arguable. It underlies the design of our questionnaires and forms the basis for the remaining material presented in this book.

For purposes of questionnaire design, I have defined structure broadly and somewhat loosely as the operating environment of the individual, those factors that impinge on his ability to move or function in specific ways within this world. These structures include the respondent's own bodily environment—his age, sex, health status, ability to move, race, and so forth—and his mental or learning environment, such as his reading level, specific mental skills and abilities, and his knowledge level.

Structures also include the spaces or confines within which a person moves or lives his life. These spaces progress in openness from his car, home, town, state, and geographic region to his country. Other important structures that confine, channel, and direct human behavior are the political, economic, climatic, and social boundaries within which the respondent lives and operates.

Obviously, some of these structures are now routinely enunciated on questionnaires, especially the demographics of age and race or ethnic background. The assumption has been that one's race or ethnic background is an important explanatory variable affecting behavior and attitude. While not being labeled as *structural*, these types of questions in fact identify some aspects of the person's bodily environment. However, many important structures affecting behavior and attitude go beyond these rudimentary demographics, and a calculated inclusion of them in overall questionnaire design is essential to understanding the meaning of respondent answers.

Some types of structures guiding behavior cannot be asked directly on questionnaires, but must be built in as a fundamental part of the data analysis. Population fluctuations are one example.

The severe drop in the birth rate in the United States during the past ten years, which may or may not be known to individual respondents, is causing a decrease in the need for teachers and schools. This has resulted in harsh competition for existing teaching vacancies and denial of tenure to qualified teachers. It has also led to job security issues and militant teachers' unions. Presidents and admissions directors of most colleges and universities must now concentrate on marketing, as the schools now compete to maintain enrollment levels rather than merely selecting the most desirable applicants from an overflowing pool of aspiring students. A typical survey among teachers may identify large areas of discontent, militancy, alienation, and feelings of insecurity which result not only from their immediate job, but from the larger ebbs and flows of population fluctuations and their impact on schools. Just because the teacher is not conscious of these larger structural changes does not mean that such changes do not play an important role in affecting his behavior and attitudes.

Why are structures important?

They are important because they explain and substantiate human behavior patterns in greater depth than examination of ephemeral attitudes can ever do. Structures provide the context that makes respondent answers meaningful or meaningless. Structures are important because they identify and influence *long-term* trends in human behavior that cannot be identified through respondent testimony alone. I can obtain respondent testimony about attitudes toward work, housing, and the family, but the drop in population growth, based in part on the introduction of effective contraception, forms the structure underlying attitudes toward and increases in the female work force, increases in the divorce rate, and changes in housing patterns.

While women will answer a questionnaire about their attitudes and interest in pursuing a career, all of their answers are a reflection of a basic structural change that they are probably not conscious of, but that now gives them the opportunity to reflect on alternative life-styles. Effective contraception has made it possible for women to pursue lifetime careers, which demand long-term commitment, predictability of time, and personal control unhindered by random, unplanned pregnancies. The ability to work for substantial periods of time, measured in years rather than months, has freed women, made them more financially independent, more in control of their own economic lives. Even this financial independence is now limited by a basic structure—the clustering of women in the lower paid, traditional female jobs, such as teaching, nursing, and clerical work. The greater wage-earning capacity of women has in turn led to demand for apartments and homes for women outside the traditional male-headed household, a phenomenon rarely known and not socially countenanced two hundred years ago. It allows women and men to have attitudes toward "equal pay for equal work," "equal credit laws," and "equal distribution of marital property," which simply would not have had any foundation in reality fifty years ago, as shown by the lack of laws in these areas. In the eighteenth century in the United States, each married woman bore an average of almost eight children before completion of her child-bearing years.[2] Regardless of her attitudes toward wage earning, no woman in this position could possibly have realistically considered a "career" as we know it today.

Planned pregnancies lead not only to lower birth rates but also to lower death rates for both babies and mothers. Women and their children live longer. While sociologists and psychologists adduce many theories to explain the increased divorce rate in the United States, one major consideration surely must be that nowhere in the previous 5,000 years of human history were husband and wife routinely expected to live (or be alive) together in close quarters for forty years or longer, a completely realistic possibility today. Men died in wars, from accidents, from plagues in the prime of life. Women died in childbirth. In preindustrial societies people lived no more than thirty-five or forty years on the average.[3] Any person who lived beyond age forty-five was considered an older person within the context of the times, but today such a person is in "mid-life crisis" and facing at least thirty productive years ahead of him, an entire lifetime compared with preindustrial societies.

In 1910, of four couples newly married, only one in four

2. Peterson, *Population*, p. 532.
3. Ibid., p. 10.

would survive as a couple to celebrate a fiftieth wedding anniversary. In 1950, of four couples newly married, *three* out of four can expect to survive as a couple to celebrate a fiftieth wedding anniversary. This is a massive *structural* change affecting marriage, child rearing, and career practices. Only against this type of change can present attitudes be realistically assessed and the depth of present social change gauged. Lack of conscious knowledge of these changes does not mean that they don't significantly alter individuals' behavior, perceptions, and even values.

How I became aware of the importance of structures

I am giving a rather detailed discussion of how I came to be aware of the issue of structures in questionnaire design, because it illustrates the broad theoretical type of reading which I find to be invaluable in an understanding of human nature, and also because it emphasizes that questionnaire writing is not only a technical skill, but a state of mind based upon openness to new ideas and the ability to see patterns in apparently widely disparate pieces of information.

My realization of the importance of physical structures in human endeavor resulted from the conjunction of two completely isolated and apparently unrelated pieces of information. The first was the American publication of Fernand Braudel's *The Mediterranean and the Mediterranean World in the Age of Philip II.* [4] While reading this book, I was grappling with the analytical problems posed by a study of the fast food market, the second event which helped me see the importance of structures in human behavior.

Fernand Braudel is a French historian. As an historian, he has been concerned with the task of conveying "simultaneously both the conspicuous history which holds our attention by its continual and dramatic changes—and that other, submerged history, almost silent and always discreet, virtually unsuspected either by its observers or its participants, which is little touched

4. Fernand Braudel, *The Mediterranean and the Mediterranean World in the Age of Philip II* (New York: Harper & Row, 1972.)

by the obstinate erosion of time." His approach to the study of history has been that "resounding events are often only momentary outbursts, surface manifestations of these larger movements and explicable only in terms of them."[5]

I believe the same is true of human behavior and attitudes. They are often mere surface manifestations of larger, structural movements beyond the control or even the consciousness of individuals. Examples of these larger structural movements are population growth and decline; climate and weather changes; communications patterns and media; transportation patterns and modes; the relationship of cities to suburban and rural areas; city size as it affects communications; food supply and trade; and profound economic changes and dislocations, such as inflation, deflation, trade balances, and shortages of imported oil.

Perhaps all of this sounds too global, if not absolutely irrelevant to the design of questionnaires, but in fact the importance of physical structures in human behavior cannot be ignored. Its relevance to survey design was demonstrated to me during the analysis of data I gathered for a study of the fast food restaurant market, while I was reading the Braudel book.

This study of the fast food market was being conducted for security analysts, and the purpose of the study was to predict the future of the fast food market. I had worked closely with the clients developing a brief but very concise questionnaire, which tried to anticipate all the possible reasons why people might or might not eat at fast food restaurants. During the report writing stage, dissatisfied with the way the report was developing, I discussed my first draft with my colleague, Caroline Weymar, who had once been a financial analyst. Her reaction was characteristically blunt. She simply glanced at the first three pages and then blurted out, "This doesn't tell me what I need to know. I don't care whether 50 percent of the people say they like such and such a restaurant very well. That doesn't tell me what I need to know about the market potential for that industry or that company. I can't use that type of attitudinal information to analyze the growth potential of a stock!" But what kind of information could be used?

We began to view the data structurally, and, fortunately, I

5. Ibid., p. 16.

had almost inadvertantly included questions on the questionnaire which would allow this type of analytical approach. What factors, excluding attitudes, would influence whether or not a person eats at a fast food restaurant?

1) Accessibility. How many people living in the United States live within three miles of a fast food restaurant? How many fast food restaurants are located within three miles of 90 percent of the U.S. population?

2) The number of meals that could possibly be eaten there per week. For most people, twenty-one meals per week is about the maximum number they can possibly eat. How many of these meals could reasonably be eaten at a fast food restaurant?

3) Family structure. Does the household have two wage earners? How many children live in the household? Do households with children eat at fast food restaurants more often than households without children? Are these types of households increasing or decreasing as a percentage of all U.S. households? What is the average number of people per household who eat at fast food restaurants per week? Is this type of household increasing or decreasing as a total percentage of U.S. households?

4) Individual characteristics. What types of individuals most frequently eat at fast food restaurants? Are they increasing or decreasing as a percentage of population? This includes age groups, ethnic groups, single versus married.

5) Income. What is the disposable income available to these people? Is this level of disposable income increasing or decreasing as a percentage of total income?

6) Physical mobility. Do older people who are less physically mobile eat out as frequently as do younger people?

7) Population density. What is the role of population density in patronage of fast food restaurants? Do people living in densely populated areas eat at such restaurants as often as people in rural areas?

Notice that none of these questions is an attitude question. None is hypothetical or projective or psychological. All are extremely concrete and "structural."

How to incorporate structures into questionnaire design

In the hypothesis development phase the first area of concentration should be structures. As mentioned above, questions about structures may or may not actually be included as questions on a questionnaire, but all possible major structures affecting behavior and attitudes should be identified and used to analyze the data to know "what you've got."

Hypotheses regarding structures can be listed by spheres leading from the largest to the most personal, beginning with physical structures located outside the immediate household or neighborhood. In the fast food study, changes in weather (summer versus winter) affecting eating-out habits was one hypothesis. In a bank marketing study, as another example, the location of specific bank branches and their distance from respondent households; the number of branches within a given radius; and the existence of drive-in windows, walk-up windows, and automatic teller machines are all structures that may affect attitudes toward banks, bank selection, and bank usage by different subgroups of the population.

The physical structures of greatest importance usually concern such items as number of outlets and accessibility in terms of distance and types of available transportation. Seasonal changes are also important. Other structures outside the household are communications networks. In a national study of the nutritional outreach program among the elderly, church attendance proved to be one of the most important communications networks affecting knowledge of and attendance at congregant meal programs for the elderly.

Communications networks explain wide variance in perceived employment opportunities and actual employment opportunities among key subgroups of the population. Low-income, low-socioeconomic-status groups tend to use newspaper want ads as a source of information about employment opportunities. However, the higher paying, more prestigious jobs are often not advertised in these want ads. People learn of these types of jobs through the "old boy network" and word of mouth at cocktail parties, luncheons, and so forth. Thus, it becomes a vicious cycle, with members of low-socioeconomic-status subgroups constantly being recycled into lower paying jobs because of their limited communications networks. Women's groups, now conscious of this problem, are forming associations to begin to provide an "old girl network" to help women move into higher paying, more prestigious jobs.

The internal physical structures of large organizations may determine employee attitudes, behavior, and job opportunities. In an employee study in a large money center bank, location of branches within the center city, which was largely black, and in the suburbs led to differences in hiring and training practices and in job opportunities. Corporate management divisions within the bank had completely different employee career tracks, some of which were known to be "fast" tracks and others to be "slow." These internal management structures had become so rigid that able employees who worked in a slow track division had virtually no opportunity to transfer laterally into a fast track division because of the competition among the separate divisions for influence and autonomy within the total corporation. Supervisory employees in one division had no knowledge of jobs available in another division to which they could transfer or promote competent employees, which led to great frustration among talented employees in some of the divisions and to wide discrepancies in pay scales.

Work conditions and employment practices profoundly affect household behavior in such areas as recreation opportunity, need for more than one car in a household, need for child care and baby-sitting services resulting from night shift work or split shifts, shopping habits, and other aspects of family life.

Type of neighborhood is also an important structure which predicts or correlates strongly with a variety of respondent behaviors. We have found in analyses of voting behavior and awareness of political issues that type and *age* of suburb are greater predictors of voting behavior than income. Two suburbs, both with the same levels of income, vote entirely differently depending upon whether the suburb was built before World War II on an old commuter railroad line or after World War II in the era of the upwardly mobile, station wagon life-style.

Legal structures must also be considered, especially in industrial marketing studies. These include federal regulations in the areas of taxation and corporate write-offs, employment laws, environmental laws, and laws regarding interstate commerce. These types of laws direct or force the direction of much corporate development. Any study of the trucking industry, for instance, encounters regulations affecting load weights; disparities in these weight and size limits between states cause trucking companies to reroute or reload to meet the regulations, thus affecting their profitability and organizational growth.

The structures within an individual state may have a profound impact on all marketing approaches that can feasibly be used within that state. In New Jersey lack of a single statewide news medium, either a commercial television station or a newspaper, as well as lack of any single major city (the state has dozens of moderately sized cities, but no really dominating city), determines the strategies for allocation of media funds, election campaign strategies, and marketing plans for statewide organizations. The state's location between the heavily saturated media markets of New York and Philadelphia makes it prohibitively expensive and ineffective for most state politicians to use television to reach voters, since they must pay New York city rates and quite naturally will reach more New Yorkers than New Jersey residents. Thus, in some areas of the state direct mail campaigns can be more effectively targeted and implemented than any television campaign. The extended commuting patterns of residents to New York or Philadelphia diffuse any statewide identity, and many New Jersey residents know more about New York or Philadelphia than they do about politics in their own state.

After considering structures outside the household or neighborhood, the researcher should investigate structures within the household as the next area of hypothesis development. Need for day care often depends on the existence and proximity of grandparents, especially in Italian and other traditional extended family ethnic groups. Such families prefer to rely upon grandparents for child care rather than day care institutions. Analysis of data on the existence of children under age five and the employment or out-of-home patterns of parents, without considering the grandparent alternative, results in an inflated demand figure for day care.

Social behavior, as well as psychological factors, such as feelings of loneliness, competence, and isolation, correlates strongly with household structures, primarily whether there are one or two heads of household. Single heads of household consistently show lower standards of living in terms of income, available transportation, and communications and social networks, and this type of household structure also correlates strongly with frequent television viewing. Many social attitudes, which correlate strongly with television viewing, in effect may result from the basic structure of the household.

□ 9
Determining respondent knowledge

The effects of respondent knowledge on answers

The problem of the effects of knowledge, or lack thereof, on respondent answers results from the fundamental operating reality of public opinion polling that people will answer questions. They will answer questions on any topic, and they will answer whether or not they know anything about that topic. The "don't know" category supposedly takes care of people who do not know, but this assumption is mistaken. If people have even heard of a topic, they will presume to know and answer questions if encouraged by an interviewer to do so.

Given that people answer questions, how do we know whether these answers reflect people's actual beliefs or opinions, or whether these answers simply reflect lack of knowledge? Are people really saying, "Keep the status quo as I perceive it," or are they really saying, "I want a change"?

Knowledge is not the same as intelligence. I may not know how to perform an appendectomy, but that does not mean I am stupid. I may never have heard of automatic teller machines, but that does not mean I could not learn how to use one. I may know very little about the Palestine Liberation Organization, but that does not mean that I can't learn anything about the political history of the Middle East.

Determining respondent lack of knowledge of specific products or public issues is crucial to understanding how to change behavior or attitudes successfully. Ascertaining levels of knowledge is the essential first step, because to change behavior, you are going to have to educate people, if possible.

From a questionnaire standpoint, people can possess three types of knowledge:

1) Personal knowledge derived from firsthand experience in the situation.

2) Factual knowledge derived from reading; personal experience; or exposure indirectly through one's profession, friends, and so forth.

3) Computational knowledge, which is the ability to compute or to make arithmetical calculations, including percentaging, addition, subtraction, and comparison of costs and prices.

Personal knowledge

Personal knowledge or direct experience becomes especially important in analyzing data in the areas of consumer products, corporate image, and retail services. For example, in a marketing study for the hotel/motel industry, key personal knowledge questions include: "Have you ever stayed overnight in a hotel/motel?" "How many nights per year (month or week) do you usually stay overnight in a hotel/motel?" "Do you stay while on business trips, or while on vacation trips, or while on convention trips?"

These types of knowledge questions make it possible to obtain weighted answers. Whether they consciously design for it or not, researchers must ask themselves whether *all* answers are equally important, or whether some answers are more equal than others. Just as some respondents may be weighted in a stratified probability sample, I believe that some respondents should also be weighted on the basis of the accuracy of their answers. *Knowledge, in addition to consciousness and behavior, is one of the weights that should be used to distinguish among respondents.*

The personal knowledge questions listed above are designed to sort out people who know virtually nothing from those who know a great deal. It is a researcher and a client decision whether all answers should be treated equally, but in the event that the opinions of knowledgeable people (within the general public) should carry more weight, only identification of such people by answers to knowledge questions can allow the researcher and the client to make these important distinctions.

In short, you can sort people out through your sampling approach, and you can further sort people out by your questionnaire approach. Both are equally essential to the successful interpretation of your survey data.

Factual knowledge

Factual knowledge becomes important in the area of public policy issues. Greater knowledge may make it difficult or impossible for some people to respond to questions on such issues. People who are not knowledgeable may see the issues in a simplistic manner: "Do you favor or oppose . . . ,", but a knowledgeable person may ask, "Under what circumstances?" Failure to obtain a measure of this knowledge factor, as well as the ignorance factor, on public issues may lead the researcher to overstate the percentage of the public holding strong opinions on an issue, and may also obscure how quickly public opinion could change if a certain issue dominated the headlines and the facts became more widely known.

The analysis below was conducted by Michael Rappeport when he was working at Opinion Research Corporation, and the data come from two studies conducted by that organization several years ago.[1]

The first poll was a regional study of attitudes toward public utilities. All respondents questioned lived in regions served by publicly owned utilities. Of particular interest to the client were answers to the question, "Which of these groups do you think *should* own and operate the electric light and power company?" The answer categories from which respondents could choose were individual investors and city, state, or federal government.

1. Michael Rappeport, "The Distinctions the Pollsters Don't Make," *The Washington Monthly*, March 1974 13–15.

The results were:

Individual investors	52%
City, state, or federal government	36
No opinion	12

Thus, only a bare majority of the general public favored private ownership of utilities, and politicians might assume that there was substantial support for public ownership.

The questionnaire for this project also contained two elementary knowledge questions:

1) "Which group on this card do you think owns the electric light and power company here?"

2) "To the best of your knowledge, does any government agency regulate the profits and rates of your local electric light and power company?

Respondents were divided into three groups according to whether they answered both questions correctly, answered one correctly, or answered neither correctly.

When analyzed by these three nondemographic knowledge subgroups, respondents' answers to the question of which group should own and operate the local utility were distributed as follows:

"Who should own and operate the electric light and power company?"

	Number of Respondents	Favor Investors	Favor Government	Don't Know
Total respondents	1,546	52%	36	12
Answered both knowledge questions correctly	523	82%	16	2
Answered one knowledge question correctly	526	53%	37	10
Answered neither knowledge question correctly	497	12%	57	31

In other words, these respondents were telling the researcher, maintain the status quo. Those who know the utilities are owned by investors and regulated overwhelmingly prefer to maintain that situation. Those people who *think* the utilities are government owned and not regulated prefer government ownership—the status quo, as far as they know. Neither set of answers can honestly be construed as a call for change in the ownership of local utilities.

Another example of the effects of knowledge on respondent answers occurs in the data from a poll conducted by Michael Rappeport for CBS News on problems in the Middle East. [2] Two factual questions were asked. One dealt with how much U.S. oil usually comes from the Arab countries, and the second dealt with whether Israel had mostly gained or mostly lost territory since it was set up in 1948. The attitude question to be analyzed by the knowledge questions was: "Some people believe the Arab countries are out to destroy Israel as a nation. Others say the Arabs are not out to destroy Israel, that they are only interested in regaining the land lost to the Israelis in the 1967 war. Which do you think is true—are the Arabs out to destroy Israel, or are they only interested in regaining their land?" Note that this attitude question presupposes knowledge of Israeli territorial gains, one of the two factual questions used for analysis.

"Are the Arabs out to destory Israel, or are they only interested in regaining their land?"

	Number of Respondents	Destroy Israel	Only Regain Land	Both or Neither	Don't Know
Total respondents	1,231*	28%	52	5	15
Answered both knowledge questions correctly	351	41%	45	8	6
Answered one knowledge question correctly	328	34%	50	5	11
Answered neither knowledge question correctly	320	15%	59	4	22

*All questions were not asked of all respondents.

Notice the sharp differences in opinion between those people who knew the correct answers to both questions and those people who did not know the correct answers. Notice also that not knowing that Israel had gained land from the Arabs did not prevent people from answering "regaining the land" as the Arabs' goal.

2. Ibid.

These data do not say that the better informed people should be taken more seriously. On public policy issues the better informed people are often more passionate and unobjective from a policymaking point of view. Nonetheless, determining what people know and how it influences their opinions is essential before the researcher can present an objective, meaningful interpretation of the data for his client.

Computational knowledge

In these days of rising inflation, high interest rates, and higher grocery bills, people are constantly being interviewed about their financial status, attitudes toward the economy, rising prices, and unemployment. All of these interviews assume that people can make arithmetical computations. We have no data to support this assumption. In fact, we have quite a bit of data supporting the reverse assumption: that people cannot add, literally, and they cannot compute.

The following question was asked of a sample of the general public who have checking accounts. The answer categories were *read* to the respondents.

"If you had $1,000 in a 5% savings account, about how much interest would you earn per year on that account?"

	Respondents
$5 per year	3%
$25 per year	8
$50 per year	60
$100 per year	1
$500 per year	* (<.5%)
Don't know	27

Recall that these respondents are bank users. They all have checking accounts. They are not the lowest economic stratum of our society. Yet 39 percent of them cannot correctly guess even in this simplest of examples the amount of interest they would earn on their savings accounts. We hypothesize that this lack of computational skill accounts for the great marketing advantage that savings and loan associations have using their additional .25 percent interest rate. People simply are not able to figure out that on a $1,000 deposit the additional interest is only $2.50 per year, hardly enough to pay for the additional gasoline it takes to get to the savings and loan building.

The types of knowledge questions which can be included routinely in surveys and used as a scale to separate subgroups are usually very simple. The purpose is not to test people's knowledge, but to obtain some brief indication of levels of knowledge that relate to the topic being explored in the interview itself. Some routine types of knowledge questions I have often included are:

Regarding abortion:

> "As far as you know, is there a movement in your state to limit abortions or make them illegal for most women?"

On energy and conservation issues:

> "Has the federal government established some type of agency or department to be responsible for energy policy and practices?"

> "What is the name of the federal agency which is responsible for energy policy and practices?"

On financial and bank marketing:

> "What is the present rate of inflation in the U.S.?"

> "What is the present interest rate paid on a *regular* passbook savings account?"

On political issues:

> "What are the names of your senators? What is the name of your congressman?"

I try to design knowledge questions by thinking about the problem in the following way: if the respondent really *knew* that such and such was the case, would that probably alter his behavior or his attitude? In a jewelry marketing study if the respondent knew how much gold was in 14 karat gold versus 10 karat gold, would that make a difference in his purchasing behavior? If account users knew that differences in interest rates would result in only minor increases in their total dollars, would they be more likely to favor a new type of account with a different interest rate? If the respondent knew that a movement to eliminate legal abortions was underway in her state, would that make her more likely to become politically active to maintain legal abortions? If people really knew what the word "profit" meant and if they knew how to calculate percentages correctly, would they be more likely to support the activities of large corporations?

□ 10
The role of behavior

After consciousness, environment, and knowledge, behavior is the fourth research tool automatically designed into a questionnaire in order to deal with the problem of the meaning of attitudes—our present inability to define, measure, or otherwise accurately determine respondent potential behavior based only on what respondents can or do tell us. Behavior questions can be used in a variety of ways, all of which are aimed primarily at determining potential future behavior.

Behavior as a means of dealing with lack of consciousness

When survey researchers ask for people's attitudes or opinions, they make the following key assumptions about respondent consciousness:

1) That people *can* analyze the problem and the situation being explored in the interview. By analyze, I mean that they can see the different parts and also see how they fit into a total picture.

2) That people *do* analyze problems and situations.

3) That after they have analyzed a problem or situation, people have enough command of the language to be able to talk about or describe the problem or situation.

4) That people *will* then tell you about the problem or situation.

5) That people can project themselves imaginatively into the future and relate their present situation to some hypothetical future situation, and then they can describe their potential feelings or behavior in the new situation.

6) That they can also visualize alternative courses of action that might be available to them in the future.

7) That they can visualize the *implications* to themselves of any alternative modes of action they might take in the future.

All of the assumptions listed above presume respondent consciousness as theorized by Julian Jaynes. I have found that analysis of current *behavior* is another method of measuring and analyzing the problem of lack of consciousness among respondents.

Perhaps the best way to underline the problem of consciousness in attitude questions is to analyze individually the assumptions of consciousness underlying specific questions that have been asked of the general public on surveys. The question below has actually been used. It can be used with the first situation (of the four listed) simply to obtain people's "gut" reactions or top-of-mind responses for the purposes of developing advertising themes. However, if it is to be used to develop data for determining under what circumstances people really believe women in these categories should carry life insurance for purposes of careful marketing of products, the question raises very serious problems of respondent consciousness.

> "Here is a list of women in different situations. For each type listed, please tell me whether it is very important for her to carry life insurance, somewhat important, or of little or no importance?"
>
> 1) A woman who is the sole support of her family.
>
> 2) A single career woman over fifty years old.
>
> 3) A single career woman under thirty years old.
>
> 4) A woman who is a full-time housewife with children under eighteen.

In order to respond *consciously* to these items, a person must make several imaginative projections or narratizations, both into the future and into the past. First, the respondent will have to be able to imagine the effects of a person's death under each of the conditions listed. That is, if a woman who is the sole support of her family dies, what will then happen to that family? If a woman who is single dies, and she is over fifty, who will that affect? After trying to figure out *who* will be affected by the death of the particular woman, then the respondent will have to visualize *what* types of effects or problems that death will provoke. In the case of a woman who is the sole support of her family, the respondent will have to imagine whether that woman is married with children, or whether she might be supporting an elderly father and mother. (Family has not been accurately defined here, so the respondent will have to define for himself what he means by the word "family," which may or may not correlate with what the researcher means by the word.)

The respondent will have to guess whether the children of such a woman have alternative guardians available. More importantly, if such guardians are available, the respondent will have to deduce that insurance on the life of that woman will be necessary to pay her burial costs and estate settlement costs, and also possibly to provide money to the alternative guardians to care for her orphaned children. The respondent will then have to decide whether these orphaned children are of college age and able to support themselves if necessary, teenagers, or preschoolers, which plays a role in determining both short-term and long-term financial needs that could be provided by insurance. All of these factors must be considered before a respondent can consciously decide how important life insurance would be for such a woman.

Similar types of visualizations and projections would be necessary for the other examples provided in this particular question. Does the single career woman over fifty have an estate or heirs that she wishes to leave money to? Does she have enough savings to pay for her own burial and settlement fees? Does it even matter to her whether she leaves an estate or not?

Is the single career woman under thirty going to be interested in building an estate for potential children? Is her health good enough to establish insurability now, or can she afford to wait until she gets married? Will she ever get married or have children? Today many women decide to do neither.

In case 4, above, the respondent will have to deduce the replacement costs of a full-time housewife with children in terms of housekeeping costs, baby-sitting costs, day care costs, and so forth.

There were a total of eight such items asked about women and a total of seven such items asked about men on this one survey questionnaire. I myself do not feel competent to provide intelligent, realistic, conscious answers to these extremely complicated questions, which place severe demands on one's intelligence, knowledge, and imaginative abilities. Do you think the average person with a high school education could perform these mental tasks as well as you could? A further question in this particular study asked people for a self-assessment of their knowledge about life insurance. In the 1978 study, 59 percent admitted that they were not too well informed or not at all informed about life insurance. What does a low level of admitted knowledge do to the accuracy or meaning of the data obtained in this questionnaire?

The behavioral approach to the same study would ask a series of easily answered questions, somewhat as follows:

1) Number of wage earners in the household.

2) Number of children and/or dependents and their ages.

3) Type of insurance existing on each wage earner, if any.

4) Approximate face value of life insurance on each wage earner. ("Face value" is a problem here, and a knowledge question about its meaning would also be important to the analysis of this question.)

5) Family income.

6) Existence of a will.

7) Provisions for guardians of children.

8) Provision of financing for guardians of children.

9) Monthly housing costs (mortgage or rent) as a rough measure of replacement income absolutely necessary.

10) If only one wage earner, employability of other adults in household based on past working experience, if any.

11) Ages of wage earners or household adults.

12) Amount of cash on hand and in savings.

13) Size of home mortgage.

14) Alternative sources of aid to the family—wealthy grandparents, other relatives, and so forth.

15) Other liquid assets in the estate.

Behavior questions cannot be thought of or asked independently of the sample stratification and design and the analytical task posed by the research problem being investigated. To obtain a truer picture of what people really think or know about life insurance, the researcher should begin by stratifying his sample and using a respondent selection table or screening questions to obtain a cross-section of enough respondents in key types of household *structures,* such as married with and without children and single by specific age categories. Then the questionnaire would consist of behavior questions which could be analyzed by household structures. In this way, the researcher would obtain a true picture of what each individual household does on a projectable sample, which would then tell the researcher what people in each type of household believe, without demanding that respondents project themselves imaginatively into differing household structures and situations that they have not actually experienced. Thus, actual behavior plus sampling plus data analysis act as a surrogate for all of those attitudinal or imagination questions asked above. The data analysis would then concentrate on the problem of household vulnerability to a sudden death of a member of the household in terms of current and potential income loss, possible ways of raising cash within the household in the event there is no life insurance, and so forth.

The behavior analysis in this example becomes synonymous with respondent knowledge. We assume that people do what they know, and that if they do not know, they do not do. Behavior also acts as a measure of importance. People who have taken the maximum number of insurance steps regard the problem of financial security seriously, while those who have not taken such steps are not *conscious* of the seriousness of the problem. In rare cases, steps will not have been taken because families simply cannot afford the extent of protection they may need. Here again, however, analysis of the household's financial situation plus actual respondent behavior is a surer indicator that financial problems are the cause of low insurance coverage than respondent testimony alone saying, "We can't afford it."

As the above example shows, attitude questions which demand respondent projection and narratization simply transfer the analytical task from the researcher to the respondent. The attitude questions about insurance listed above ask the respondent, rather than the researcher, to analyze the issues and potential problems. The opposite should be true. Behavior questions provide data for analysis. The respondent can accurately describe what he does. The researcher, however, designs the sample and the questionnaire to allow the respondent to describe fully what he does, and then the researcher, not the respondent, analyzes and projects the meaning. The researcher, with the help of the client, is certainly in a better position to know all the variables affecting the purchase of and need for life insurance for any type of household. *The respondent's actual purchase of life insurance is a more accurate representation of what he believes about his life insurance needs than anything he might say in response to a direct question.* Attitude questions demanding that the respondent imagine unexperienced, hypothetical situations are often simply a shifting of the responsibility for analysis from the researcher to the respondent, a lazy researcher's way of handling difficult thinking, which more often than not provides very weak data.

None of the behavior questions listed above demands imaginative skill or projectable consciousness on the part of the respondent. These questions also place minimal demands on actual knowledge of insurance, a complex subject indeed.

Behavior versus socially acceptable answers

Behavior questions also avoid the problem of socially acceptable answers, that is, answers the respondent provides that are consistent with his perceptions of what the interviewer wants or consistent with the mores of his society. By definition, what people already do is generally perceived by them to be socially acceptable, and, therefore, behavior questions are much less likely to encourage inflated or unrealistic answers prompted by unknown or unstated but implicit social pressures.

As an example of socially acceptable answers which may not constitute reliable data, consider the answers given by three respondents to the question, "Which *one* of the following do you feel is most to blame for the energy problems the United States is having?" The three possible answers were: the consumer, the oil companies, government regulation. All three respondents answered, "the consumer." As a follow-up to their selection of the consumer, these respondents were asked, "Is there any one thing the consumer could do to really help our energy problems?" The three respondents answered as follows:

1) "Hopeless, up to the powers that be."
2) "Use of car pooling."
3) "Kids should walk more. Public transportation. Be conservative by car pooling, solar heat, insulation, turn heat down, air conditioning up."

Except for the first answer, all of the answers are socially acceptable. But what do these respondents actually do, these respondents who say "the consumer" is most responsible for the energy shortage? We do not know. The questions were not asked. Based on these answers, we could erroneously assume that the respondents are socially conscious, perhaps self-sacrificing. In fact, each respondent was asked whether he would use his car significantly less if gasoline were increased to $1.10, $1.50, $2.00, or $2.25 per gallon. All said, no, they would not decrease the use of their cars if the price went up. Although not strictly a behavior question, the fact that they would not change their behavior suggests that they have not altered their behavior. Thus, their answers indicate social consciousness or conserving behavior and attitudes, as long as it's someone else doing the conserving. Make the kids walk more.

If instead behavior questions had been asked about what this respondent has actually *done* to conserve gasoline—do his children walk more, does he participate in a car pool, has he installed more insulation or solar heat, at what temperature was his thermostat set at the time of the interview?—then we would obtain a definite view of his actual energy-conserving priorities, if any, and thus the relative importance of energy conservation in his life beyond what he says it is. The most fundamental assumption behind these types of behavior questions is that if the respondent is serious with his answers, he will not only have talked about it, he will have *done* something about it.

I have mentioned three isolated respondents, but this type of answer pattern is typical; spread over 100 respondents out of 1,000, for example, the data can become extremely soft, a cause of greater error than that associated with sampling error. In questionnaire design, as perhaps nowhere else, talk is cheap. The purpose behind behavior questions is to find out exactly how cheap that respondent talk is. Can the answers be believed, or even taken seriously, or are they all hot air?

Behavior as a means of defining sensitive problems

Behavior questions can also define sensitive issues more readily than attitude questions. For example, people may not be able to define what a "battered" child is or what excessive drinking is. Furthermore, questions on these topics will almost certainly elicit socially acceptable answers at variance with what people actually do. After all, how many people will admit to an interviewer that they drink too much or that they beat their kids? Behavior questions, while not a panacea, can provide very valuable insight into these complex issues and further refine definitions of touchy topics. As mentioned several times earlier, at this stage of questionnaire design, the design must mesh with subsequent analysis; they cannot be handled independently of one another. Some examples below indicate the relationship.

One problem encountered in a survey was to try to define "battered children" and also to attempt to learn if there was a social standard of what is legitimate and what is unacceptable punishment of children. To deal with this research problem, respondents were provided with a long list of punishments, increasing in severity as the list progressed. The respondent was asked which of those punishments had been meted out to him as a child. Then the respondent was asked whether he felt he had been dealt with too harshly, too leniently, or about right. Subsequent analysis did indeed indicate that there was a social standard of acceptable punishment unrelated to ethnic differences or cultures.[1]

1. Michael Rappeport and Patricia Labaw, "1978–1979 Title XX Human Services Needs Assessment Study," prepared for the Office of Policy and Management, Connecticut Department of Human Resources, 1979.

Another difficult word to define is "loneliness" or "isolation." Respondents cannot define it. However, the researcher can include in his questionnaire a series of behavior questions, covering such activities as going out of the home during the day, going out at night, going out on weekends, receiving telephone calls, making telephone calls, number of hours spent watching TV, ability to drive, and ability to walk. Each one of these detailed behavior items can then be included in a simple score, which classifies people into categories of high social activity, moderate activity, and low activity. The researcher, since he has defined these categories, knows exactly what is meant by his definition of loneliness without being dependent upon the spontaneous and perhaps pressured definitions provided by hundreds of respondents to interviewers. While people may argue with the researcher about his definition of loneliness, at least it is a concrete definition to argue about, with clear parameters for all to view and acknowledge. No one has to argue about what the respondents really meant when they said they were "very lonely" in response to a vague general survey question.

With answers from 1,000 respondents who have detailed their actual social behavior in terms of a series of small, but concrete, behaviors as the data base, not only is the researcher provided with a behavior-based definition of loneliness rather than a subjective definition, but he can develop norms of social activity by age groups, household structures, and so forth. Using precisely this type of series of detailed behavior questions, we have consistently learned that single heads of household with children are more likely than the elderly to suffer from loneliness or isolation.

Present behavior leads to similar future behavior

Behavior questions are particularly important in areas where potential future behavior is under study. We have little data to support the idea that people will radically change their present behavior unless some serious *structural* change forces a behavior change. For example, lack of gasoline causes people to use mass transit more. However, in voluntary circumstances people tend to grow into new behavior out of similar or related past behavior.

For example, in a study of car pooling and use of buses versus use of personal automobiles, we found that people who *already* participate in car pools are better candidates for mass transit use than people who do not. Thus, installation of buses on these same routes would be likely only to transfer people from car pools into buses, but would have little impact on transferring single car drivers into users of buses.

Similarly, banks which are concerned about effective introduction of electronic funds transfer (EFT) services have learned that people who are already using such specific automated services as automatic teller machines or who are heavy credit card users consistently show greater favorability toward and higher usage of more general EFT services when they are introduced.

When designing a questionnaire aimed at determining potential future behavior, the most important design problem is to include a battery of behavior questions detailing present behavior that is similar to or related in some way to the potential behavior under study. The most obvious example of present behavior dictating future behavior occurs in election projections. People who have voted in the past for a specific party overwhelmingly repeat this behavior, regardless of the candidate involved. This is why primary election projections become so difficult. The actual number of people voting can be predicted, but since all candidates come from the same party, accurately predicting a primary winner in a field of four or more becomes extremely difficult.

Some behavior can falsify answers

In one important area actual behavior regularly inflates answers. This area, dear to the hearts of many advertisers and politicians, concerns sources of information about a candidate or a topic. We usually advise the client not to waste his money on such a question, because people, when asked to list the sources of their information about a topic, routinely answer, "television." Since television is the most important information-disseminating medium in the United States at present, and since people spend enormous numbers of hours watching television, they automatically assume that, whatever it is, they saw it or heard it on TV.

In this case, the overwhelming behavior pattern of watching TV dictates the respondents' answers, whether true or not.

Behavior indicates what people know or don't know

This problem is similar to that of lack of consciousness. Often behavior results from what people don't know, as well as from what they do know. In this case, what people don't do can be more important than what they do. The hound of the Baskervilles is silent.

During the past few years several research firms have designed and conducted a series of energy consumption monitoring experiments. These experiments have been implemented to learn exactly how different types of households, living in identical types of housing (newly constructed townhouses), use energy, and what key variables correlate with differing rates of energy usage. As part of these studies, respondents in each household were given instruments which provided them with immediate feedback about their energy usage. This immediate knowledge of the effects of their energy usage behavior caused many households to adjust their behavior. They could see that bathing in a full tub used more energy than showering. They could see that closing draperies and curtains in the summer during the day lowered the need for air conditioning. They could see how a constant opening and closing of doors by children could substantially increase energy consumption by the constant flow of heated or cooled air to the out-of-doors. These types of experiments provide important support to the idea that much human behavior indicates *lack* of knowledge rather than knowledge.

Once again, the concomitant design of questions in terms of the subsequent analysis, in this case, analysis of lack of knowledge as indicated by current behavior, emphasizes that the researcher, not the respondent, is responsible for the analysis. Regardless of what the respondent tells you of his attitudes toward conserving energy, the experiments discussed above provide a true indication of respondent reality and priorities undistorted by lack of consciousness, lack of knowledge, social pressures, or undefined complex terms. Behavior tells a complete story. Respondent testimony provides an incomplete story.

☐ 11
Gross versus cumulative definitions: confirming the null hypothesis

This chapter draws together two themes discussed earlier: the role of hypotheses as the foundation of questionnaire structure, and the problem of the average respondent's inability to articulate, describe, discuss, or define complex issues. I have touched on the need to structure a questionnaire around the anticipated needs of data analysis, that the two go hand in hand, and in this chapter I will present a more complete discussion of one way in which questionnaire design can be integrated with data analysis.

The role of hypotheses and the problem of inarticulate respondents come together on the issue of definitions of complex or multifaceted behavior or issues. Often, if not in the majority of cases, the survey researcher is presented with a problem of definition by the client. For example, how does an "alcoholic" differ from a moderate or frequent drinker? How does a "quality" bank customer differ from other bank customers? How does a "needy" family differ from one that is not needy? How do you define "need"? How does one airline differ from another in "service"? In a broad sense, all of these research questions are problems of definition.

Respondents can usually define these types of issues only with broad, rather obvious answers. An alcoholic is a person who drinks too much or who goes on a four-day bender, passes out, and cannot remember what he did. A quality bank customer is one who deposits $1,000,000 in the bank or one who has a lot of money. A needy person is one who is crippled or cannot walk. An airline is different from other airlines if it has more planes or bigger planes than its competitors. People use price as a standard means of definition. If it is more expensive, it is better or of higher quality.

All types of social or marketing issues demand definition. On the other hand, society constantly redefines existing terms. Social need is an obvious example. Fund-raising organizations, such as the United Way, frequently conduct surveys to determine how people now define "needy" compared with definitions used in past years. Norms of acceptable behavior also constantly change, and new norms are established. A person considered an "alcoholic" by today's standards may have been regarded simply as a heavy drinker a hundred years ago. Surveys are often used as tools to establish these new norms of behavior.

Norms of behavior change as a result of such disparate structural changes as the aging of the total population, inflation, and a larger number of competitive organizations. Philanthropic organizations particularly face changes in giving and donor behavior as a result of these types of structural changes in the society at large. Large inner-city churches may now have huge endowments but small congregations as a result of former wealthy city dwellers moving to the suburbs. The older, established philanthropic institutions, such as the Red Cross and Easter Seals, face severe competition for funds from newer fund-raising organizations with quite different interests and appeals: the American Civil Liberties Union, the Sierra Club, the National Abortion Rights League, and so forth. Small donations given in response to door-to-door solicitations and mass mailings have been replaced by larger "pledges" solicited through television campaigns and careful analysis of the attitudes and interests of special constituencies. Yet these more complex philanthropic behaviors cannot be defined simply using such transparent questions as, "Do you donate money to charitable organizations?" or "What kinds of people do you think most need help in our society?" The real issue does not concern overall donor behavior, but specific types of donor behavior based on extended patterns of giving.

The crux of these definitional problems lies in the null hypothesis. In all forms of research, hypotheses are best phrased as null hypotheses. A family is not needy. A person is not an alcoholic. An airline is not different. Refuting a null hypothesis is often relatively easy. A man who drinks a quart of whiskey a day is an alcoholic and refutes the null hypothesis that he is not an alcoholic. An airline that has one of its planes crash every day is not a safe airline. A person who maintains a $5 deposit in his savings account and has no checking account is not a quality bank customer.

The problem here lies not so much with refuting the null hypothesis, but with confirming it. On a continuum of complex behaviors, where is the dividing line between a safe and an unsafe airline, between a heavy drinker and an alcoholic, between a child who is punished and one who is battered? The nature of the proof in these cases is to *define* that the object or person or household is *not* what it or he appears to be.

Definition concerns relative importance or relative seriousness or relative intensities of behavior. Respondents can usually recognize the obvious major act or behavior that defines a social problem, and survey researchers often depend on this simplistic recognition to define the extent and severity or importance of an issue. When a parent beats a child so severely that his legs and arms are broken, most people would agree that this constitutes child abuse. These are gross definitions. However, problems or issues can also be identified through accumulation; that is, a long series of small, repeated acts conducted steadily for a sustained period of time can cumulatively equal a major social problem. These types of small, cumulative characteristics or behaviors can also define a quality bank customer, and they can also define differences between airlines.

Small, cumulative behaviors can be used to confirm the null hypothesis in the absence of obvious proof to refute it. However, to define the seriousness, importance, or differences of an issue, the researcher must design the questionnaire to gather not only the obvious gross definitions of the problem or issue, but also the small behaviors or characteristics that, in accumulation, indicate major importance, seriousness, or differences.

I have listed below both gross definitions and cumulative definitions which have been used to solve major survey research problems of confirming or refuting the null hypothesis.

Example 1

Hypothesis: Households with incomes under $25,000 per year are not quality bank customers (that is, "profitable" bank customers).

Profitability for a bank can be defined using gross definitions or examples (a customer with a $1,000,000 deposit) or cumulative definitions (a customer who uses a variety of bank services and/or maintains high balances and/or generates fee or interest income). Questions were asked to obtain data for both the gross definition and the cumulative definition, as follows:

1) Number of checking accounts per household.

2) Control over a business or partnership account.

3) Types of accounts or services used at main bank.

4) Level of switching of bank accounts due to dissatisfaction.

5) Balances in savings and checking accounts.

6) Use of savings certificates.

7) Use of savings bonds.

8) Use of home mortgage, and home ownership/rental.

9) Variety and number of other financial services used.

10) Use of major credit cards.

11) Household income.

12) Age of respondent, and existence of multiple wage earners in household.

Households were scored, usually with one point per item. Statistically, the list was long enough so that no one item carried enough weight to distort the score. Based on this scoring system, 10 percent of the respondents qualified as "high-quality" bank customers, confirming the old banking axiom that 20 percent of a bank's customers give it 80 percent of its business. That 20 percent consists of the 10 percent high-quality customers plus those medium-quality customers who score within one or two points of being high quality. [1]

1. Mary Ann Pezzullo, "Quantifying Quality," prepared by R L Associates for United Jersey Bank (Princeton, New Jersey), 1978.

Example 2

Hypothesis: This person is not a problem drinker. [2]

Demographically, problem drinkers are indistinguishable from occasional drinkers. An occasional drinker is self-defined as one who only drinks up to three alcoholic beverages a week. A frequent drinker is self-defined as one who has four or more drinks per week. A problem drinker is simply self-defined as one with a drinking problem. Thus, the definitional problem is to define a frequent drinker and a problem drinker *nondemographically*, which cannot be done only through the use of gross definitions based on overall quantity of alcohol consumed or level of alcohol in the bloodstream.

A series of questions was developed to learn where people drink, when people drink, and behavior after consumption of alcohol—three series of questions in all.

Location of drinking
1) At home?
2) At a friend's home?
3) In a bar or pub?
4) In a restaurant?

Occasions for drinking
1) At parties or other social occasions?
2) Before dinner?
3) While watching TV?
4) While doing chores around the house or yard?
5) Wine with meals?
6) Before or with lunch?
7) After-dinner highball or cordial?

Behavior after consumption
1) Driving and drinking?
2) Ever been fired for drinking or threatened to be fired for drinking?
3) Someone in your family ever left you because of drinking?
4) Ever threatened to leave you?

2. Michael Rappeport and Patricia Labaw, "The Public Evaluates the NIAAA Public Education Campaign," prepared by Opinion Research Corporation for the Alcohol, Drug Abuse, and Mental Health Administration, Public Health Service, U.S. Department of Health, Education, and Welfare, July 1975.

5) Someone in your family ever complained about your drinking?

6) Ever arrested by police for intoxication?

7) Has a doctor ever told you that drinking was injuring your health?

8) Ever wake up and not remember what you did while drinking?

Notice that all of the questions are simple, discrete behavior questions. There are no attitude questions here, no hypothetical questions. Most of them are not likely to threaten a respondent because they are embedded in a long list. The analysis will focus on cumulative effect rather than place great significance on one direct question.

The data collected from these questions allowed the analysts to define alcoholism in two distinct cumulative ways:

1) Alcohol abuse is that use of alcohol that causes an individual to behave in ways the individual would not normally wish to behave, either in terms of a major personal event or a series of small but continual alcohol-related personal events.

2) Alcohol abuse is the drinking of more than certain amounts of alcohol (consumption patterns). This definition may be measured in terms of single occurrences or patterns of behavior over time, but in each case the behavior of interest is the amount drunk.

Both definitions of alcohol abuse are necessary for a complete understanding of socially unacceptable drinking behavior. They are also essential for the design and implementation of educational campaigns to cope with drinking problems in the United States, where perceptions of the existence of a "drinking problem" tend to emphasize the single blatant episode (falling down drunk) rather than the chronic, low-key but constant, drinking that does not result in major observable episodes. None of these definitions depends upon the respondent's self-appraisal, although each can readily be correlated with respondent self-appraisal to define what the respondent means when he describes himself as a drinker. These measures are sociological rather than physical measures. They do not depend on levels of alcohol in the blood to determine alcoholism.

Example 3

Hypothesis: A happy person is not housebound.

In studies of social service needs researchers often assume that feelings of psychological well-being correlate negatively with loneliness, and that isolation breeds low psychological well-being. Yet we have found that at least one measure of isolation—getting out of one's home—does not correlate to a significant degree with adverse scores on Norman Bradburn's negative psychological well-being scale.[3] In fact, we identified four distinct subgroups in the population based on a combination of an isolation scale and the Bradburn scale of positive-negative psychological well-being:[4]

1) People who get out of their homes virtually every day and are rarely depressed, lonely, or bored.

2) People who don't get out of their homes any more often than three times a week but are also rarely depressed, lonely, or bored.

3) People who get out of their homes vitually every day but are still frequently depressed, bored, or lonely.

4) People who don't get out of their homes more often than three times a week and are also frequently depressed, lonely, or bored.

This may appear to be an academic exercise, but millions of dollars in federal money are distributed on the assumption that being alone equals loneliness and that being with people equals not being lonely. For example, based on the analytical conjunction of the two scoring systems, both based on series of items rather than single items, we learned that elderly homeowners are housebound but not necessarily unhappy; blacks, renters, and the transitory poor are more likely to be unhappy but not housebound.

In the area of product or service marketing a similar development of series of items combined with scoring techniques yields fruitful marketing options. For example, while safety may be perceived as the most important feature of an airline, all airlines

3. Norman Bradburn, *The Structure of Psychological Well-Being* (Chicago: Aldine, 1969).

4. Michael Rappeport and Patricia Labaw, "1978–1979 Title XX Human Services Needs Assessment Study," prepared for the Office of Policy and Management, Connecticut Department of Human Resources, 1979.

may be perceived as being equally safe. Safety does not provide a marketing edge. However, using a series of features associated with airline services (meals, on-time arrivals, ease of check-in and check-out, in-flight services, and so forth), respondents can classify individual items according to how important each item is to them in the selection of an airline, and also whether they perceive any differences between airlines on these items. Through subsequent analysis, classifying items according to high importance/high difference, high importance/low difference, low importance/high difference, and low importance/low difference, the product marketer receives concrete information about the relative importance of each factor to potential customers in their selection of an airline. This scheme also immediately identifies for the marketer those aspects that can realistically be emphasized in advertising (those that are classified as high importance/high difference between competing airlines) with potentially the greatest results.

All of the issues discussed in this section depend upon a conjunction of two (or more) scales and subsequent analysis to define the issue or problem. A quality bank customer is defined by what he has (money balances) and by what he does (use of multiple financial services). The heavy drinker is defined by quantity of alcohol consumed, frequency of drinking, and number of adverse drinking-related incidents. A socially needy person is defined by level of personal mobility and social contacts and by Bradburn's scale of well-being. Airline differences are defined by the rated importance of a variety of services and by perceived differences among airlines on delivery of services.

Most of these scales utilize behavioral items or, as with the Bradburn scale and the airline example above, self-perceptions and value judgments about services. All of the definitions depend upon the cumulative results of a series of items rather than upon one key definition or one key question. Through analysis of a series of small behaviors, norms can be obtained that can be compared with norms obtained from outside sources or with norms obtained within the survey itself. In all cases, these types of questions can be answered readily and usually unambiguously by the respondent without depending upon high levels of respondent consciousness, respondent knowledge, or respondent verbal communications skills. However, to be successful, the researcher must know in advance that he wants a cumulative definition as well as a gross definition. He will have to hypothesize in advance what factors contribute to a cumulative definition of his problem or issue and plan his analytical and scoring techniques in advance.

☐ 12
Routing and leading the respondent

In the previous sections of this book, I have discussed the theoretical or mental concepts a researcher must keep in mind when designing his questionnaire. Questions to be included in a questionnaire should determine levels of consciousness; levels of respondent knowledge; actual respondent behavior, which indicates both knowledge and value structures; and questions which confirm or deny the null hypothesis, primarily behavioral questions that are subsequently scored to obtain definitions of complex terms or concepts.

In this chapter I begin to discuss the layout or format of the questionnaire, again from a conceptual point of view. There are three considerations in the actual layout of a questionnaire on paper. The first is what I have called formatting: the presentation of the questions in such a way as to facilitate interviewer progress from question to question and to allow efficient keypunching of the data. Questionnaire format has been touched on in other parts of this book and will not be discussed further here.

The second consideration is that of *routing*, which is a mechanical process affecting the respondent as he progresses through the interview. Routing includes such items as exclusion questions to eliminate some respondents from a succeeding section of the questionnaire; sequencing of questions to maintain respondent interest and participation in the interview; and sequencing of questions to avoid mind sets, the most common example of which is position effect.

The third consideration in questionnaire layout is that of *leading* the respondent. Leading has a very bad name in the survey research profession. Leading can be defined as the "unavoidable" education of the respondent. To ask a respondent about any topic is to educate that respondent. I believe that this education, since it automatically occurs during the interview, should not be haphazard; it can be controlled, and it can be used in subsequent data analysis as an integral part of the research process aside from specific question wording.

Routing the respondent

In the most common routing the questionnaire resembles a downward funnel. The respondent is funneled from a series of general, nonthreatening questions down to more specific, more personal questions. However, there are other routes or pathways which can be designed to serve a specific research function, and these alternative routes are discussed below.

Routing to avoid refusals and terminations

The first and most common way that researchers route respondents is to take them, literally, into the interview itself. Thus, the first goal of routing the respondent is to prevent refusals. Refusals can occur because the respondent thinks he is not interested in the topic, or because the topic is perceived as too personal or too sensitive. The introduction to the questionnaire is designed to respond to both of these problems. Ideally, the introduction should whet the respondent's appetite and pique his curiosity about the nature of the questions to follow without simultaneously arousing fears about them. A political questionnaire may be introduced as a study of "important issues facing your community." A bank marketing questionnaire may be introduced as a "study of new financial services." I always try to use as brief an introduction as possible, which gives the respondent little opportunity to refuse.

In government-sponsored studies special problems arise with the introduction. Specifically, current federal privacy regulations require fairly detailed discussions of the respondent's right to refuse to be interviewed. Here in particular, careful wording is required so as to clarify the respondent's right to privacy without frightening him.

The next step in drawing the respondent into the interview is to write a general question touching the topics to be covered, yet broad enough so that the respondent feels comfortable and reassured in answering it. For example, political questionnaires, before getting into specifics about candidates and campaigns, may begin with a broad question about the most important social problems in the community. I do not regard these initial broad questions as "throwaways." I always try to use a question that will provide solid information for my study or which can be used for subsequent analysis, but which nevertheless provides some content of interest to the average respondent.

The introduction and the first one or two questions are used to anticipate terminations due to the sensitivity of a topic. If you plunge too directly into many sensitive topic areas, the respondent will often terminate, especially in a telephone interview. The goal here is to obtain as much information as possible and establish rapport before creating a situation which may provoke a termination.

Terminations can, however, be used as an analytical tool of special importance when dealing with sensitive issues. In the study of attitudes toward abortion I began the questionnaire with all of the demographics (which are usually left until last), progressed through topics of sex education, and then began the abortion section. I coded the questions where terminations occurred and analyzed the respondents who terminated by the key demographics obtained at the beginning of the questionnaire. In effect, I analyzed nonresponse. I also coded the respondent's stated reasons for terminating, if they were given. I found that those people who terminated when I reached the abortion section of the questionnaire tended to be older, low-income women. The demographics of this group matched those of respondents who completed the interview but who tended to oppose abortion most strongly, and I believe that the terminations in most cases expressed opposition to abortion, rather than opposition to the interview itself, especially when combined with such responses as, "I don't care to discuss this any further" or "I don't believe in it."

Routing to identify specific subgroups

In many studies not all questions need to be asked of all respondents. Identification of specific subgroups is achieved by routing respondents through questionnaires. In political questionnaries you can route respondents by asking them whether they are Democrats, Republicans, or Independents. Depending on the answer, an individual respondent may be asked a series of questions about issues involving either the Democratic or Republican political parties.

In a study of sex education in the public school system the researcher may be very interested in the attitudes of the total public, so all respondents may be asked for overall attitudes and experience with the public school system and sex education courses. However, respondents with children in the public school system may be of particular importance, because they are currently directly involved with the problem. Therefore, a screening question may be asked along the lines of, "Do you now have children attending the public schools in this county?" A negative answer routes respondents either to a new section of the questionnaire or to the demographics. A positive answer leads respondents to a series of questions directly related to their position as parents of schoolchildren who must confront teenage sexual activity and need for sex education. A similar type of exclusion may occur in a study of social service needs. The researcher may want to know overall public support for social services but then identify particular subgroups of the population in terms of their specific need for services. A series of routing or exclusion questions will identify each subgroup. For example, an exclusion question can be asked regarding drinking habits, followed by a series of questions relating to identification of a drinking problem; an exclusion question can be asked about family structure to identify single people living alone, which would be followed by questions about personal mobility and social contacts. On any given question a portion of respondents would be routed past the succeeding set of questions, and a portion would be routed through the succeeding questions. Thus, the questionnaire acts as a series of filters through which some groups pass while others are detained or sifted into a different topic area. Here is an example of a typical format that I use.

HAND RESPONDENT CARD A

1. On this card are four kinds of people. Please read me the number of the statement that best describes you.

1 ABSTAINER–**GO TO Q.____**
2 OCCASIONAL DRINKER
3 FREQUENT DRINKER
4 DRINKING PROBLEM

IF RESPONDENTS ARE 2, 3, 4, ABOVE, ASK:

2. For each of the occasions I will read you, please tell me whether you often, sometimes, or never are likely to drink on that occasion.

   a. Drink at parties or other social occasions.

Often	*Sometimes*	*Never*
1	2	3

Routing to break up mind sets

One major questionnaire design problem results from the need to use lists of statements. For each statement on a list, the respondent is asked either to agree/disagree or to make some other judgment. For example, in a questionnaire used in a study of attitudes of the elderly toward the police, respondents were asked about numerous items appearing on several lists. These concerned the perceived safety of their homes (including house, yard or grounds, garage, elevator, hallways, nearby public parks, buses, and shopping areas); types of actions taken to improve personal safety (installation of locks, alarms, window grilles, or lights; purchase of a dog or firearms; and so forth); items used to describe the police (speed of arrival, sympathy to the problems, honesty, efficiency, and other image items); and problems for which the police may be called (person suffering from chest pains, lost pets, obscene phone calls, home repair problems, problems with neighbors, vandalism, drinking problems and personal quarrels, information needs, and so forth). Many other lists were also used throughout this one interview. Lists are often essential in questionnaires because they allow a respondent to cover a great deal of material very quickly. However, they create a questionnaire problem of mind set. The very process of going through these long lists of items causes the respondent to begin to answer by rote rather than with any degree of thought about each item. The interviewer may inadvertently encourage such automatic response in order to hasten the interview and to prevent the respondent from becoming bored with the process itself.

To cope with this problem of mind set, the rhythm of the lists needs to be interrupted to jar the respondent into consciousness of his answers and to prevent his developing patterns of response that do not reflect his real attitudes or behavior. To interrupt this rote response, the lists need to be distributed throughout the questionnaire and to be separated by other types of questions that call on different mental faculties of the respondent. Answer categories should also vary, if possible, from list to list, so that conceptually the respondent is asked to make different evaluations or responses. For example, some statements can be phrased as agree/disagree statements; others may call for levels of respondent familiarity (very, fairly, not too, or not at all); others may ask the respondent to rate (excellent, good, fair, or poor); and still other statements can be treated as true/false statements. When designing these lists, the researcher often has the option of phrasing statements in a variety of ways, and one rule for determining statement phrasing should be to interrupt mind set.

Within each list, statements can also be worded either positively or negatively and randomly distributed within the list to provoke the respondent into thinking about his answers.

To analyze the effects of patterns of response, a split questionnaire technique can be used, with one form's statements being phrased in one way, and the statements on the other form being phrased in the opposite way. For example, on form A the statement could read, "Teaching children sex education at school will lead to more teenage sex before marriage." The statement on form B could read, "Teaching children sex education at school will not lead to more teenage sex before marriage." Half of the sample would receive form A and half would receive form B. After completion of the interviewing, the answers to the two forms of the questionnaire can be examined to see if the percentages of respondents agreeing with the positive form and disagreeing with the negative form are approximately equal within sampling tolerances.

Another way of dealing with the problem of mind set on long lists is to repeat an item or two from a list farther on in the questionnaire to see whether the respondent answers the two items consistently. Or the respondent's answer to one item can be repeated to him, and then he can be asked to explain his answer to ensure that he truly does understand and is conscious of his own meaning.

Routing to avoid position effect

The second most common reason for routing a respondent through a questionnaire is to avoid position effect. In other words, you may not want a respondent's answers to reflect or be influenced by the questions that preceded them. An obvious example is that you would not ask a series of questions about various issues affecting the public schools, such as incidence of drug use or existence of racial problems or fights, and then ask people what they think are the most important problems facing the public school system. The respondents would simply play back "drugs" and "racial problems" as the most important issues in the schools.

However, position effect can also be used as an important research tool. In a recent study on family planning, questions were first asked about familiarity with specific organizations in the field, followed by questions about the functions performed by such organizations, including counseling, abortion referrals, provision of low-cost abortions, and education in the schools. At the end of the interview, the respondent was asked to name any organizations he could think of working strongly to support abortion. The client organization was named by only a very small percentage of the public, even *after* it had been named and discussed in the interview, confirming and emphasizing the other data in the questionnaire which indicated a very favorable image of the organization combined with limited knowledge of its activities.

Leading the respondent

When a respondent has completed an interview, he is not the same respondent who began the interview. He has been educated. The process of the interview itself educates the respondent and can cause an alteration in attitudes and behavior as a result of the respondent's increased consciousness. This is unavoidable. In a recent image study of social service organizations respondents were asked from what sources they had heard or read about the organization being studied. Under "other answer," a respondent had candidly replied, "from this interview." Interviewers often receive comments from respondents at the end of an interview, saying, now that they've heard of the product or the problem or now that they understand more of the issues, they have changed their mind or plan to change their behavior.

Conscious leading of the respondent by the researcher is used to try to duplicate the effects of information, communication, and education on the respondent in real life. For example, the researcher may try to measure the effects of certain advertising themes or messages, or he may try to measure the effects of certain types of information introduced by the opposition's candidate during the course of a political campaign.

Systematic introduction of new pieces of information surrounding an issue will lead the respondent to clarify and define further the boundaries of his favorability or opposition on an issue. A respondent may favor withdrawing troops from West Germany provided that such and such a course of action is also taken. Rarely is favorability or opposition absolute. Therefore, the researcher needs to learn the limits of this opposition/favorability, and the introduction of new information as the interview progresses is one way of learning the depth of feeling on an issue.

Shown below is a sequence of questions which could be asked to determine the extent of favorability or lack of favorability toward a new financial service.

1) Ask for overall favorability toward a new type of bank financial service card.

2) Ask for favorability if this card would cost the user $3.00 per month.

3) Ask for favorability if this card would provide a line of credit up to $500 to the user.

4) Ask for favorability if the user of this card would be required to leave all his cancelled checks in the custody of the bank.

5) Ask for favorability if use of this card meant that the customer would receive 2 percent discounts on purchases of goods and services.

6) Ask for favorability if use of this card meant that the customer's checking account was immediately debited when a purchase transaction had been completed.

7) Ask for favorability toward this card compared with ordinary all-purpose charge cards.

8) Ask for overall favorability again.

As the above example shows, the researcher can take advantage of this process of interview education to achieve greater understanding of the motivations and environment conditioning the respondent's attitudes and behavior. At the beginning of the interview the respondent can be asked for overall levels of knowledge of and favorability toward the issue or product. In a study of alternative power sources respondents could be asked at the beginning of the interview for overall favorability toward nuclear power, coal-fired generating plants, and oil-fueled generating plants. Then the interview could progress through a section that deals with the problems surrounding nuclear plants, such as thermal pollution, radiation discharge, nuclear accident, and disposal of radioactive wastes. For coal power generation, topics could include strip mining, air pollution, water pollution from mine wastes, deep coal mining and associated problems of accident and health hazards, disposal of fly ash, and thermal pollution. For oil-generated plants, issues of oil spills, offshore drilling, and imports of oil and associated financial and political problems could be introduced. At the end the respondent could once again be asked for comparative favorability toward the alternative sources of power generation. His beginning and ending answers could then be compared to see whether his favorability changed after he had been educated to the issues surrounding each power source.

It may be argued that this biases the respondent's answers, but in the real world publication of the actual issues affecting power generation has indeed resulted in changes in people's attitudes and behavior. Leading the respondent through the issues using the questionnaire is our way of learning in advance how increased publicity will affect our respondents. Without this knowledge, we cannot honestly say what the base level of favorability or opposition to an issue is, and public opinion changes will appear to be volatile. This volatility does not reflect badly on the public, but it does reflect the researcher's failure to understand and anticipate the effects of increased publicity on the public's behavior and attitudes.

Another example of deliberate education of the respondent and its effects on respondent answers is a survey concerning a Democratic congressional race in which three candidates were running before the primaries. One particular district included three important geographic subareas. At the beginning of the questionnaire a standard trial heat question was asked:

"If the Democratic primary election for congressman were held today, and the candidates were _____, _____, and _____, who would you be most likely to vote for?"

The results among "very likely voters" were:

Candidate 1	28%
Candidate 2	16
Candidate 3	30
Undecided	26

After this trial heat, respondents were told that the second candidate lived in a specific town in one of the geographic areas, that he had been mayor of that town, and that he had successfully resisted a specific type of corruption while mayor. These were all facts that the candidate believed he could successfully communicate to the voters during the course of his campaign.

Then another trial heat question was asked, with results as follows:

Candidate 1	24%
Candidate 2	28
Candidate 3	30
Undecided	18

In product marketing studies similar procedures of education can be used, specifically, testing potential ad themes that might motivate respondents to try the new product. The total questionnaire becomes a process of education deliberately designed to reveal as much as possible about what information factors carry the most influence with respondents to motivate behavior change or attitude change.

One important educational feature often used is introduction of pricing variables. People rarely understand or know the extent of associated costs on either social issues or products or services they routinely use. While price changes are not an infallible means of understanding human behavior, they do provide important guidelines which help measure the extent to which costs are important to respondents.

The key to understanding the effects of education on the respondent lies in deliberately designing the questionnaire to anticipate and measure educational effect by obtaining a measurement of attitudes at the beginning and then again at the completion of the interview, which will document whether a change has occurred. For example, such a technique used on a questionnaire concerning abortion shows little change in attitudes. At the beginning of the series on attitudes toward abortion, people were asked, "Overall, what are your feelings toward allowing legal abortions in the United States? Do you favor strongly, favor somewhat, oppose somewhat, or oppose strongly allowing legal abortions in the United States?" At the end of the question series on abortion, people were asked, "All things considered, how would you summarize your feelings about abortion? PROBE: Do you generally favor or generally oppose abortion, and why do you say that?" People know where they stand on this widely publicized and very personal issue. When answers were compared between the two favorability questions, no movement from favorable to unfavorable or from unfavorable to favorable had occurred. On issues of less personal concern or knowledge, however, attitude change can occur simply as a result of the different arguments or points of fact built into the questionnaire itself.

Leading to determine the parameters of the issue

Respondents can be led through a questionnaire deliberately to define the parameters or dimensions of an issue. This technique is best suited for important social or political issues that are often oversimplified in public opinion polls. Again, this technique should commence with a broad measurement of attitudes or opinions *before* the questionnaire has progressed very far, that is, before the education process has begun or gone very far. The technique consists essentially of presenting alternative choices and progressing through a series of more and more difficult or concrete choices, forcing the respondent to set limits to his opinions and to think about the issue under study from a variety of points of view. A complex issue deserves this approach. Any simple approach based on only one or two questions can completely mislead the researcher and his client.

An example is the Panama Canal series of questions discussed at the beginning of this book. As mentioned then, public opinion remained remarkably stable as long as respondents were asked only about overall favorability, using one question. When another dimension of the problem was introduced, the right of the United States to intervene in the case of an attack on the canal, public opinion reversed on the issue. In fact, a series of questions defining these different parameters would have given a clearer picture of public opinion on the issue, as the switch outlined above indicates. The series could have been written along these lines:

1) Overall measure of favorability or opposition to the canal treaties.

2) Overall measures of knowledge about the canal (simple questions, such as where it is located, whether the largest ships can now go through it, what the present political arrangements of the canal are, and so forth).

3) A progression of questions along the lines of favoring/ opposing the treaties:

    a) If the United States had rights of intervention.
    b) If the United States maintained joint rights of operation.
    c) If a United Nations force were sent to moderate all issues between Panama and the United States.
    d) If the United States could maintain a small armed force in the canal area.
    e) If the United States only used the canal for X% of its total shipping cargo to and from the United States.
    f) If the total U.S. dollar volume of shipping using the canal were only X% of all U.S. shipping dollar volume.
    g) Other alternatives or dimensions of the issue.

4) Final measure of favorability or opposition to the canal treaties.

A similar procedure could be used for the issue of sex education in the schools. For example:

1) Obtain overall measure of favorability or opposition to sex education being taught in the schools.

2) Determine whether the respondent would maintain that favorability/opposition if:

a) Sex education classes were taught as part of a total physical hygiene class.

b) Sex education were taught as part of a biology class.

c) Sex education were taught as part of a family living class.

d) Sex education were taught emphasizing only *physical* aspects of reproduction.

e) Sex education were taught emphasizing *moral* aspects of sexual conduct.

f) Boys and girls were taught separately/together.

g) Boys and girls were taught only with parental permission.

h) Boys and girls were taught only at X ages.

3) Obtain final measure of favorability or opposition to sex education being taught in the schools.

Notice that all of the above techniques of leading and routing a respondent depend on a series of integrated questions rather than solo questions. This approach assumes that the researcher is responsible for directing the respondent for a variety of reasons: for screening and subgroup identification, to interrupt patterns of response and mind sets, to help define the meaningful parameters of an issue, and to measure the effects of education upon respondent answers. The questionnaire is written keeping this need for respondent direction in mind. All of these techniques give the researcher a better understanding of his respondents and provide a means of determining more accurately actual respondent behavior and attitudes, and the factors that may change them. In this way, leading the respondent actually provides more meaningful data rather than acting as a source of "bias," the big bugaboo of both clients and researchers. Certainly, we are presenting biased data to our clients if we have failed to explore the effects of the questionnaire raised above. Pretending that we are not leading the respondent, that a questionnaire is totally disinterested and objective, can and does result in presentation of misleading or dishonest data to our clients.

If the approaches outlined above are used, a questionnaire can become more like a controlled experiment, with the experimenter responsible for its direction. Physical scientists do not simply allow their experiments to occur randomly or undirected and then expect to obtain meaningful results. Social scientists should behave no differently. While I sincerely believe that questionnaire writing will never become a strict science, this does not preclude the need for systematic use of some basic principles of research. The effects of the researcher's direction of the respondent can be determined and analyzed and included in the interpretation of the data. Without this effort to narrow the respondent down, to focus or filter his responses, the researcher can only obtain a nebulous cloud of answers that provide no insight, no guidance, and no predictability of behavior under varying conditions. Worse, the researcher has no means of measuring the impact of his own questionnaire on the respondent's answers.

The other side of this coin is that leading the respondent is dangerous and can deliberately bias the data in favor of a preconceived point of view. For this reason, I prefer to use these leading techniques only for *factual* or *knowledge* types of questions, rather than for attitude questions. In other words, I try systematically to introduce new *facts* to the respondent rather than new *feelings*. The following are examples of attitudinally leading questions which I would generally try to avoid:

1) "Tell me if you agree or disagree with these statements:

a) Most men are better suited emotionally for politics than are most women.

b) Most men are better suited emotionally for jobs in large corporations than are most women.

c) Most men are better suited emotionally for life in the army than are most women."

2) "I am going to name some problems faced in this country. For each one, I'd like you to tell me whether you think we're spending too much money on it, too little money, or about the right amount

a) Space exploration programs.

b) National defense.

c) Protection of the environment.

d) Help for the physically handicapped.

e) Help for battered children."

3) "Would you have any objection to sending your children to a school:

   a) Where a few of the children are blacks?

   b) Where most of the children are blacks?

   c) Where most of the children are blacks but your child would not be bused across town?"

Another safeguard against problems of bias through leading is the requirement by the American Association for Public Opinion Research that the entire series of questions in a poll be published when any part of the results is released for any reason.

This problem of bias and leading plagues all people engaged in this field, partly because a charge of bias is so easily leveled at the profession by opponents of a particular study or by media seeking headlines. Because bias is so complex, anyone can cry "bias" and make life hell for the survey researcher. I believe that the best defense against such charges lies in the following steps, which I have emphasized throughout this book:

1) A thorough examination of *all* hypotheses underlying the study. Nothing can be assumed. There should be no unexamined assumptions in the study regarding the goals of the client, the nature of respondents, or the questionnaire design and question wording.

2) Definite articulation of the study's goals. This is the best defense against people who abstract small parts of a study and use them as examples of bias. Since a study, to be effective, must be thoroughly integrated—designed around its goals, which determine the sample, the questionnaire, the data-processing plan, and the report—abstraction of parts of a poll and attempts to apply these parts to some other aspect of the problem or to attack them apart from the total poll is unethical behavior by the attackers.

3) Recognition and dissemination of the ideas that a poll is not neutral and that it is not all-encompassing. The profession does itself a disservice to describe a poll as "objective." A poll is *selective*, and it results from a process of selection regarding goals, sample, questions to be asked or deleted, analysis to be included or deleted, and so forth. Limited resources and limited time demand such selectivity. However, the rationale behind the selectivity should be clear and defensible in terms of the study's goals.

4) Public disclosure of the poll in its entirety, including the project's goals. The total context of the poll must be available. Only in this way can charges of bias be refuted.

Needless to say, all of these steps demand severe intellectual honesty on the part of both clients and researchers.

☐ 13
Question formulation

All of the previous chapters of this book have dealt with question-naire construction as a totality, emphasizing the importance of multiple questions working together to build a body of knowledge, sequence of questions to deal with routing and leading of the respondent, and types of questions (behavioral, knowledge, structural). This chapter treats the next level of questionnaire construction: actual question formulation.

Basically there are three types of questions:

1) Open-ended questions which allow the respondent to give a totally free answer.

2) Open questions with precoded answer categories. This type of question appears completely open to the respondent and allows the respondent to give a totally unstructured answer, but the interviewer codes the answer into prestated answer categories provided by the researcher on the questionnaire.

3) Closed questions. The actual answer categories are provided to the respondent, and the respondent is expected to choose the answer category which comes closest to or best represents his feelings, beliefs, attitudes, opinions, behavior, or knowledge of a situation.

In this chapter I will discuss the advantages and disadvantages of these three basic types of questions, and how they can be used to understand and predict respondent behavior.

Open-ended questions without precoded answer categories

In *The Art of Asking Questions* Stanley Payne lists several varieties of open-ended or free-response questions, specifically:

1) Introductory questions to help the respondent settle into the interview.

2) Suggestions or recommendations for action on a specific topic.

3) Follow-up for further elaboration of preceding questions.

4) Reasons why, usually in response to a preceding choice question.

5) Argument questions.

6) Knowledge or memory tests.

7) Sources of respondent knowledge.

8) Factual information.

While these classifications may be helpful, the more important point is that these types of questions (open-ended) are *indispensable* to a thorough understanding of complex issues and topics. The main advantage to free-response or open-ended questions is that they are the only way the researcher can give the respondent the opportunity to "have his own say." Presumably, although this is often forgotten, the main purpose of an interview, the most important goal of the entire survey profession, is to let the respondent have his say, to let him tell the researcher what he means, not vice versa. If we do not let the respondent have his say, why bother to interview him at all?

In spite of this vital role, open-ended questions now receive a very bad press in the survey profession. Over the past several years, the disadvantages of free-response questions, especially coding costs associated with processing and tabulating answers, have apparently seemed overwhelming to survey research firms. Many questionnaires are now designed without any totally open questions (questions without precoded answer categories).

As a result of this trend, I believe that coding costs have now been transferred into data-processing costs. To substitute for open questions, researchers lengthen their questionnaires with endless lists of multiple choice and agree/disagree statements, which are then handled by sophisticated data-processing analytical techniques to try to massage some pattern or meaning out of this huge mass of precoded and punched data. I have found that a well-written open-ended question can eliminate the need for several closed questions, and that subsequent data analysis becomes clear and easy compared to the obfuscation provided by data massaging. However unsophisticated actual respondent answers may be, if questions have been well formulated, either open or closed questions, the answers of the respondents will be closer to the truth of actual respondent attitudes and opinions than any preformulated, pseudoscientific scaling items devised by researchers and manipulated by computer operators. I advocate free-response questions because this is the *only* way I can really let my respondent "have his say."

When precoded or closed questions are used to the exclusion of open-ended questions, the researcher demonstrates one or more of the following research attitudes, all of which suggest poor research behavior:

1) I don't want to know what my respondent thinks.

2) I want to know what my respondent thinks, but I can do a better job of phrasing his statements and thoughts than he can.

3) I can anticipate *everything* my respondent thinks or feels in advance, and thus I need ask only precoded questions.

4) I don't know how to code my respondent's answers meaningfully, even if I do let him tell me what he means.

5) I can't phrase the question well enough to get a meaningful answer from my respondent.

6) I don't want to be bothered coding my respondent's answers, because it is either too expensive or too time-consuming.

Obviously, I do not believe that all questions on a questionnaire should be open, but several types of issue complexity make such questions especially valuable if not absolutely indispensable to a complete understanding of respondent attitudes.

Uses of open-ended questions
The primary purposes of open-ended questions as I use them are to learn:

1) How the respondent actually defines a preceding closed question. For example, when the respondent says the energy

shortage is "very serious," what does he mean by those words, and what objective data, if any, does he use to indicate that there is a very serious energy shortage?

2) To learn how involved or concerned the respondent is with an issue. Is the respondent merely answering questions, or does he understand the issues in a meaningful sense?

3) To define ambiguous terms. For example, in a study for a Jewish volunteer organization devoted to the cause of Zionism, members were asked, "What does Zionism mean to you personally?" The following types of answers were given, any one of which has important implications for the organization's leadership in its formulation and presentation of membership goals and materials:

"A homeland for the Jewish people."

"Supporting Israel. Insuring the right of Israel to exist."

"It means to be a good Jew."

"Jewish liberation movement."

"A belief in the state of Israel that conflicts with many American ideals."

"The central meaning of my life."

"Being a Jew is one thing, but being a Zionist is another. Zionists are very pushy, and I don't like that."

Open-ended questions and complex issues

Open-ended questions provide absolutely indispensable insight into how respondents interpret complex but apparently single-issue questions. For example, "What are your feelings toward abortion?" is phrased as a single-issue question—abortion. However, the issue of abortion itself is not single; it is multifaceted. It is an issue with many ambivalent positions. It deals with the issues of killing and murder, it deals with the issues of mental and physical health, it deals with the issues of sexual morality, it deals with the issues of the economics of poor families, and it deals with issues of world overpopulation and limited food supply, among others.

Another example of a complex issue that appears to be a single issue is favorability toward Israel. A person could favor the idea of a Jewish homeland, the idea of providing opportunities for the

Palestinians, and the immigration policies of Israel, and yet could oppose the religious conservatism of Israel, the country's policy of settlement on the West Bank, and so forth.

Any major social issue, such as the arms race and nuclear armaments, installation of nuclear power plants, coal mining and land use issues, and distribution of federal money to different population groups, contains many facets that preclude a simple yes or no, favorable or unfavorable answer by respondents.

These complex issues can be handled in two ways. First, the issue can be broken into several questions, each one embodying one discrete aspect of the issue. This approach is valuable and necessary. However, to be completely effective it depends on very extensive prior knowledge on the part of the researcher to insure that all of the important aspects have been covered in the questionnaire. The second approach is to use open questions to get the respondent to verbalize his ambivalence, if it exists, on the issue.

It is true that many respondents may simply not be able to discuss a complex issue. However, you will have a positive, statistically reliable measure of this nonresponse when you have actually given the respondent an opportunity to say the equivalent of "I don't know" or "I won't say." When you use open-ended questions, you will not provoke easy, glib, or unthoughtful answers from the respondent as readily as you will by using precoded answers that you have articulated and provided in the questionnaires. The problem of refusal or inarticulate answers will occur frequently only on those issues about which people indeed know nothing or show virtually no interest. On important issues, such as abortion or the energy shortage, people may have ambivalent feelings, but this very ambivalence results from their having thought about it and having deep feelings about it, all of which lead to extensive answers to open-ended questions. (In fact, we had to instruct interviewers working on the abortion study to prevent the respondents from talking too extensively, which did become a problem because of interest in the topic.)

Measuring intensity of feeling

Open-ended questions allow the respondent to indicate the depth of his feelings on controversial issues. Depth of feeling does not show up accurately on a standard scale used to measure it. For example, in an abortion study respondents were asked a routine overall favorability question about abortion—strongly or somewhat favorable, or strongly or somewhat opposed, to allowing legal abortions. Following this, they were asked to summarize their feelings about abortion.

In hundreds of interviews respondents answered that they generally *favored* abortion (either strongly or somewhat),

    1) To save the life of the mother.
    2) In cases of incest or rape.

Similarly, hundreds of other respondents on the same study answered that they strongly or somewhat *opposed* abortion. When asked the follow-up open question, "Why do you say that?" they answered:

    1) To save the life of the mother.
    2) In cases of incest or rape.

Thus, in the case of favorability toward abortion, without this open-ended follow-up question, the researcher would be in serious danger of *overstating* public favorability toward abortion based on the favorability scale provided to respondents. The open-ended follow-up allowed the respondents to report the limits they had placed on their answers of strongly or somewhat favorable. On the other hand, the researcher would also have been in danger of overstating opposition to abortion. This open question allowed the respondents to report the limits they had placed on both favorability and opposition, which in this case happened to be exactly the same limits.

This open question also allowed other ambivalent people to state their position more accurately:

    1) "I am personally opposed to abortion, but it is a necessary evil and poor people may need it."
    2) "I favor abortion, but not to be used as contraception, not to be used just like walking into a store."

This great middle ground of conflict and ambivalence underlies any major public issue and only free-response questions will allow it to surface.

Open-ended questions to define terms
and identify lack of understanding

Open-ended questions can indicate to the researcher whether the respondent has understood the terminology used by the researchers. Such questions may reveal not only a problem of "generic" words, but a problem of phrasing of questions which the researcher may not have anticipated. In a bank study the respondents were asked to describe why they felt their particular bank was "superior" to other banks in the area. One respondent answered, "Because my bank is not humble." Granted, this is not a significant source of respondent error, but it brings the researcher back to reality, an awareness that he has to be more conscious of the multiple meanings of the words he routinely uses in his questions. This type of misunderstanding of commonly used words can cause as much distortion of your data as sampling error, but you will never know it unless you allow the respondent to define key words for you.

Open-ended questions can be used to ask for definitions of concepts or ideas commonly used in advertising or marketing approaches. I have found that definitions of such concepts vary by socioeconomic subgroup and other important demographic and marketing variables. Nonetheless, perhaps one of the most important uses of open-ended questions is to give the respondent the opportunity to tell you when he does not understand your terms. When asked to define "fair pricing" of bank services, many respondents candidly answered, "I don't know what you mean by that." Similar answers were given when people were asked to define "competent" bank service. Thus, far from lying, many people will tell you what they don't know if you will give them the opportunity.

Coding of open-ended questions

One important criticism of open-ended questions emphasizes the difficulty of "constructing meaningful variables for statistical analysis."[1] I believe that this problem reflects the standard practice of entrusting the coding operation to nonprofessional clerical staff. This is no knock on these people, but with rare exceptions,

1. Don A. Dillman, *Mail and Telephone Surveys* (New York: John Wiley & Sons, 1978), p. 88.

meaningful coding is extremely difficult and demands professional levels of knowledge of the problem being researched, the client's information needs, and the issues the open question is attempting to answer. Coders are rarely fully acquainted with all of these issues, and thus they have no sense of appropriate selectivity in their coding, no sense of priorities. The solution for coders is thus to code everything as finely as possible, whether it is meaningful or not.

In my years of working with coders I have found that the task itself becomes so tedious, so boring, that coders tend to reach the lowest common denominator of coding—word coding. That is, when the coder spots certain words in a phrase, he automatically slots it into a category without really attempting to decipher the content, or the context, or the total meaning of the respondent's answer. With rare exceptions, this type of coding provides little insight to the researcher and does not lead to construction of meaningful variables for data analysis. Of recent studies I have worked on, only one case, a banking study, stands out as an important example of the value of word coding. When respondents were asked about fair pricing of bank services, a very large number simply answered, "free checking accounts." I deliberately kept this word code separate from all other answers to obtain an exact count of how many people see this as the criterion for fair pricing of bank services. This issue of free checking was very significant to the client's problems with marketing new retail products; that is, if a bank offers a free service once and then retracts it, this creates credibility and marketing problems for the bank in the introduction of subsequent new products.

Rather than word coding, the objective is to code *concepts*, and this presents an entirely different coding task. The more complex the concepts, the more complex the coding task, and it seems unreasonable to ask that minimum wage coders be expected to perform Ph.D.-level coding. In our office professional staff members handle virtually all of the coding, and we do not consider it a misplaced use of professional time. In fact, our professional staff members have been subjected to gibes and teasing by other professionals in the field because we do our own coding and do not hire coders to do it—a form of professional snobbery that often results in providing the client with inferior work. We find that preliminary coding by professional staff members prepares the researcher for writing the subsequent interpretive report. In fact, by reading hundreds of verbatim responses, the researcher can interpret the data, can understand its meaning and significance, much more deeply than he can by reporting simple percentages attached to rather vague answer categories.

The concepts used to form a code depend upon a thorough understanding of the client's information needs. This, as well as insuring meaningful reporting of respondent answers, is one of the most important criteria for developing code concepts. Unfortunately, in many large research firms, when an account person deals directly with the client, comes back to the shop and tells the researcher what the client's problems are, and then that researcher in turn tries to tell the coder what the client's problems are, something is definitely lost in transmission. This is why coded questions so frequently provide mushy data. The problem lies not so much with the question form itself—open-ended—but with the way in which these types of questions are processed within the research firm.

Concept codes need not be voluminous. The simplest concept code can consist of two punch categories: "respondent understood the question" and "respondent did not understand the question." This type of code was used in a recent study of interest-bearing checking accounts. The client wanted to know if the term, "NOW accounts," had become generic to the general public. We first asked a closed question, "Have you heard or read anything about a new service called a NOW account?" For those respondents who answered yes, we then asked an open question, "As far as you know, what is a NOW account?" About 20 percent of those who had heard of it had no idea what it was, according to their free-response answers. We had no interest in coding and did not need to code the different categories or descriptions of lack of knowledge provided by these respondents, only whether they indicated a basic level of knowledge of the principles of such accounts.

This raises another important problem with coding as it is usually handled: misplaced precision. When I was taught coding principles, I was told to try to keep the "other" answer category to less than 10 percent and lower if possible. This results in creation of too many codes that are too fine to provide usable information. It also encourages word coding instead of concept coding. I fail to understand why it is necessary to provide fifteen categories of respondent answers when five will provide the information the client really needs, even if this selectivity does result in a 25 percent "other" answer category. Certainly, the client will find four or five *actionable* code categories much more meaningful than twenty categories that account for every answer but only satisfy idle curiosity about the wide variety of possible respondent answers.

In a recent bank marketing study for a trust department close acquaintance with the client's marketing problems led to the following brief concept codes in response to the question: "Why would you choose that person/organization for your executor?" PROBE: "What were your most important considerations?" The concept codes were developed from a marketing viewpoint, not from the viewpoint of precise accounting of all respondent answers. These codes were developed to help the client design advertising themes, and also they were developed to help tell the bank what approaches their account executives should use in dealing with potential trust customers. The concepts developed and percentage of respondent answers applying to each were as follows:

1) Importance of knowledge, expertise to
   potential customer.   16%

2) Importance of history, habit, past relationships with the bank.   3

3) Importance of trust, honesty, confidence
   in the bank.   37

4) Importance of personal knowledge of client's
   needs, intimacy with client.   33

5) All other answers   29

(Answers add to more than 100% because of multiple answers.)

Analysis of these four basic concept codes by key demographics, including a financial sophistication scale and a financial assets scale, provided extremely meaningful variables for statistical analysis and, more importantly, helped provide the client with concrete marketing approaches which could be used for different market segments.

Notice that there were only *four* basic codes in response to this question. As mentioned before, I believe the greatest problem with most coding is that coders separate answers into too many fine categories simply to account for all the available answers. This also results from an inability to distinguish the meaningful concepts from the meaningless ones from the client's point of view. Only the researcher has enough knowledge of the client's needs to make these distinctions, unless he sits with the coder day after day to insure that the coder thoroughly understands the coding issues. Furthermore, emphasis on coding minutiae is instrumental in making coding the expensive, time-consuming operation it usually is, but does not have to be.

Open-ended questions with precoded answers

Although many surveys apparently include open-ended questions, the benefits of such questions are lost because researchers insist on inserting precoded answers for the interviewers to circle during the interview. Such precoded answers present many opportunities for serious error to be introduced into the survey results because they:

1) Depend upon the interviewer to listen very carefully to the response.

2) Depend upon the interviewer to *interpret* the response correctly.

3) Depend upon the interviewer to *interpret* correctly what the researcher intended to be included under the precoded answer categories he provided.

4) Depend upon the interviewer to circle the correct answer category.

Expecting the average field interviewer to make this complex set of judgments while maintaining the attention of the respondent is also inviting serious error. This type of error introduced into the survey findings can never be identified or measured. The researcher must simply take a leap of faith that the entire interviewing process has been handled accurately. This blind assumption makes the researcher's distorted concern over sampling variance seem ludicrous on its face.

Shown below is an example of precoding demanded of interviewers in a study of unemployment. A typical respondent could have answered the stated question, "Why didn't you look for a job?" with the following answer:

"I had a new job lined up, but my mother fell down the stairs. I had to take care of her, and when I went back to that job, they said I couldn't have it. I didn't have enough schooling. I haven't been looking around much anymore because I've had asthma."

Now, using the actual answer precodes given below, how would you code the above answer during the course of a one-hour interview without losing the attention of your respondent? Would you code only one salient part of the respondent's answer? Would you code his mother's illness under "family reasons" or under "health or disability"? If you code only salience, as interviewers often do, you underrepresent some answers and overstate others.

CIRCLE ALL RESPONSES THAT APPLY:

Had a job/new job to begin	1
Expected to be recalled or have hours reinstated	2
Believed could not find a job	3
Believed no suitable jobs available	4
Retired/not interested in working anymore	5
Not employable, nontransferable skills, unskilled	6
Return to school/obtain training	7
Not employable: age	8
Family reasons: day care/family care, spouse objections	9
Health or disability	10
Vacation	11
Other (specify)	12

A further serious problem with precoded answer categories is that the researcher assumes he is competent, qualified, and knowledgeable enough to provide all the relevant and meaningful answer categories in advance. In fact, there is absolutely no way that I, the researcher, can clearly anticipate and enunciate every possible nuance of feeling or answer that may be provided by 1,000 people interviewed on a national probability sample poll. My respondents will tell me something I don't know, if I let them, and if I am truly a researcher rather than a propagandist. Can I really anticipate the appropriate answer categories to the question, "You said you favored abortion to save the life of the mother. Why is the mother's life more important than that of the fetus?" This is an open-ended question that gives the respondent an opportunity for wide latitude of response that has not been strictly imposed from the outside by the researcher, and careful reading of responses and coding of these answers by the researcher will provide analytical insight that cannot be obtained in any other way.

Closed questions

Closed questions have become the mainstay of survey researchers. They appear to be inexpensive to administer and to process because they demand no coding and no extensive handwritten answers by interviewers. They also allow easy statistical analysis. However, closed questions have a serious drawback. In many cases the researcher cannot really know what the answers actually meant to the *respondent*. In other words, the researcher treats the data from closed questions as representing how people really feel, when in actuality he is reporting data on how people answer when forced to answer a question. The major criticism leveled against open-ended questions, that they are too difficult to answer, leads to the opposite and equally valid criticism of closed questions, that they are too *easy* to answer.

In an open-ended question situation two points of interpretation are brought out into the open for critical examination if necessary by both the researcher and the client:

1) The inferences that the respondent made about what the question actually meant to him.

2) The inferences made by the researcher about what the respondent's answer actually meant.

Verbatim answers, even allowing for the inadequacy of interviewers in writing down complete verbatim answers, permit these inferences to be seen. In closed questions, however, the inferences are obliterated, although they are still there. Because they are hidden, the researcher can ignore them. In an open-ended question the verbalization of the answer by the respondent allows the researcher (and the client) to peer into the respondent's head and learn whether the respondent understands the researcher's question and whether the researcher understands the respondent's answer.

When the researcher asks a closed question, he has no way of knowing whether the respondent understands the question, nor does he know whether the respondent actually understands the answer categories, and consequently he does not really know the meaning of the respondent's answer.

I have emphasized throughout this book that a questionnaire is a means of communication between the researcher and the respondent, that the ultimate goal of every questionnaire should be to provide a means of letting the respondent tell the researcher truthfully and as accurately as possible what the respondent knows, thinks, feels, and does. In closed questions this two-way communication process may be clouded by the following types of misunderstanding:

Researcher to respondent

1) The researcher does not say what he means (wording problems, multiple concepts per question, poorly phrased questions, poor hypotheses).

2) The researcher says what he means, but it is open to interpretation (a specific word may have several different meanings, a concept may have several different aspects).

Respondent to researcher

1) The answer categories provided by the researcher may not be adequate to allow the respondent to express the depth or breadth of his true feelings, behavior, or knowledge.

2) The answer categories provided by the researcher may mean something different to the respondent than they do to the researcher.

3) The respondent may never have thought about the issues being raised by the question, and therefore his answers will be completely uninformed or misinformed.

4) The respondent may not care about the issues being raised by the question, and therefore his answers may reflect salience rather than any concern or thought of his own.

These objections may not be serious if the researcher and client intend to treat the data frivolously. However, in most studies I have worked on the client intends to take the data very seriously indeed, and therefore he wants and needs answers that reflect some true state of reality. However, most instruction in the art of writing questions is directed only to one side of the above equation: *how the researcher communicates to the respondent.* Equally important is *how the respondent communicates to the researcher.* Closed questions can disguise the fact that there may be no communication going on at all, just an exchange of questions and answers.

As a researcher, you take it for granted that you know what the respondent means by his answers because you wrote the questions, and you know what the questions mean and what you expect in the way of rational answers. Closed questions enhance this illusion, but open-ended questions often bring the lack of communication out into the open.

Closed questions can entail three kinds of problems which are also common to open-ended questions:

1) Finding words to convey accurately what you mean to the respondent.

2) Finding words that the respondent understands on a grammatical level.

3) Understanding what the respondent means when he says, "very favorable" or "not too familiar." Ostensibly, this type of meaning is handled by rank ordering, but as shown on the abortion questions discussed earlier, rank ordering does not always convey a uniform gradation of meaning.

Here is an image question often used in retail bank marketing studies. These types of closed questions provide some of the best examples of the inherent weaknesses of closed questions. They are extremely easy for respondents to answer and provide meaningless data.

> "Now I would like to get your impressions of the various banks and savings institutions in this area. Please tell me which bank or savings institution comes to your mind first when you hear the following statements. There are no right or wrong answers; we just want to find out how you feel from what you know or have heard."

	Precoded Bank Names			
	Bank 1	Bank 2	Bank 3	Bank 4
Largest	1	2	3	4
Most friendly	1	2	3	4
Most progressive, modern	1	2	3	4
More for the man in the street	1	2	3	4
Best teller service	1	2	3	4
Most active in civic affairs and community projects	1	2	3	4

Going through each one of these image items (there were twenty-one in all), ask yourself the following questions about each item. Then you will see that, first, the researcher has not found words to convey an unambiguous meaning to the respondent and, second, that the researcher has not found words that the respondent can be depended upon to define or understand in the same way as the researcher.

1) What does *"largest"* mean to me? Does it mean that the bank has the tallest building on Main Street, that the bank has more branches than any other bank in the state, or that the bank has more assets than any other bank? If 70 percent of my respondents say the client bank is the largest, what does that mean? Further, do my respondents think it is good or bad for a bank to be the largest?

2) What does *"most friendly"* mean to me? As discussed earlier, friendly to some people means a smile and a hello, or knowing you personally by name, or showing special care and concern about solving your problems. If I tell my client that 35 percent of my respondents see his bank as "most friendly" what does that mean? If 35 percent of my respondents see my client's bank as not so friendly, what do I recommend to my client? Should all the tellers learn everyone's first name?

3) What does *"progressive, modern"* mean to me? It could mean that the bank provides stereo equipment as gifts instead of dishes. It could mean installing automatic teller machines in grocery stores. It could mean providing checks with Miró or Klee paintings reproduced on them.

4) What does "man in the street" mean? Does the average American use this term to describe himself? Do you? Maybe it means someone is the victim of a hit-and-run accident or a drunk.

If 45 percent of my respondents name my client's bank as one which does more for the man in the street, it may mean they think the bank has a resuscitator handy at the information desk for anyone who collapses in the street.

Now carry this exercise to the next step. As a customer, which banks in your area would you apply these answers to? Would you apply them only to the banks you actually use, or would you quite objectively recall the major competing banks in your area and include them in your consciousness as you answer each image item above? Would you just randomly spout off the name of some bank to please the interviewer and get off the phone more quickly? This raises a third issue concerning closed questions: what does the respondent have in his head when he gives you an answer? Does his answer reflect genuine thought, random response, or politeness to the interviewer, or does it mean what it appears to mean—that he does indeed hold a discernably different image for each competing bank in his geographic area? Researchers assume (but in fact should simply pray for) the latter case.

After you have asked yourself these questions of meaning from a respondent's point of view, the next step is to ask these questions from the client's point of view. Of what earthly value are the answers to these questions in helping a bank client solve his retail marketing problems? In fact, at a recent meeting this was precisely the question we asked our bank client when he urged us to trend the above image questions on a statewide retail banking study. If we find that 68 percent of respondents say that their bank is the largest, how does that help the bank's marketing efforts? We have data from other studies that indicate that for young business managers, largeness is an asset, but for the elderly in small towns, largeness is a liability. The bank can't do a great deal to become large in any sense of the word. It cannot go out and immediately build a series of new branches. It is not going to add five stories to its downtown office building. It cannot increase its assets 15 percent during the next year. So how does this information help the client?

Further discussion with the client revealed that in fact he had one serious issue that he wanted to know more about. As deliberate policy, the bank does not immediately institute new products and services simply to be the leader in the community.

It is not a large bank (does not have the most assets), and it is concerned about the faddishness of many new services, as well as their potential profitability or lack thereof. Was this slower pace of introduction of new services hurting the bank among its present customers? This is an answerable question, but it cannot be answered by using the twenty-one image items from the image study which had been conducted three years earlier.

While wording, meaning of respondent answers, and ability to act on the study findings are all serious issues affecting closed questions, actual statistical analysis of closed questions presents a much more serious research problem, which I have never seen discussed. That is, statistical variables can be constructed and reported for these closed questions which encourage people to give answers when they do not know what they are talking about. Statistical handling of closed questions gives equal weight to people who know what they are talking about and to people who do not. Why should researchers knowingly lump together knowledgeable and unknowledgeable, caring and uninterested respondents? Researchers as a rule do not willingly lump together old people and young people, blacks and whites, poorly educated and highly educated respondents. Yet they automatically lump together disparate answer groups, and the result—an averaging out of answers—falsifies the survey results as surely as sample bias.

In fact, survey researchers can legitimately be accused of overemphasizing the importance of asking unbiased questions in order to evade the problem of creating bias by treating all respondents equally in the statistical distribution of answers across closed-question answer categories. Researchers refuse to treat some answers as more important than others. Rank ordering on a simple Guttman scale does not distinguish important answers from unimportant ones. In fact, Dillman's very criticism of open-ended questions shows this unwillingness to grapple with respondent variance:

> Perhaps the biggest disadvantage is that these kinds of questions can be very demanding. People are asked to recall past experiences, reorganize them, and find the terms with which to express them. The task of creating and articulating answers is difficult for most respondents, especially those with low educational attainment or who lack experience in communicating ideas to other people.[2]

2. Dillman, *Mail and Telephone Surveys*, p. 88.

The implied next step, which is in fact what closed questions do, is to fill in this respondent lack, deliberately give the respondent the "answers," and then treat these answers as though the respondent had given them.

Closed questions are conceived of as performing a "counting" function. All answers must be included, and all answers must be counted as equal, whether they are or not. This is why data based solely on closed questions can be so unstable. *All answers are not equal.* As discussed and emphasized throughout this book, some respondents are *conscious*, some are *knowledgeable*, and some are *involved*. People who show these characteristics tend to be more stable in their attitudes toward an issue than those who do not. When only attitudes or salience are measured, without measurement of the above three respondent characteristics, the data are unstable and can be influenced by many extraneous variables. One major goal of this book has been to emphasize this need to view some respondent answers as more valuable than others in solving the client's problems, and to provide approaches to eliciting answers of superior value.

In an article entitled "Interviewing Changes Attitudes— Sometimes" Bridge et al. ask, "Does the mere asking of questions motivate a respondent to form attitudes which were previously absent, or to change the direction or intensity of extant attitudes?"[3] The authors conclude, among other things, that when issues "are already salient to respondents, no attitude change or information seeking is stimulated by the interview. . . . But when issues are poorly understood, respondents are encouraged to rethink their opinions so that their beliefs about the importance of an issue will come into line with the importance that the interviewer evidently ascribes to the issue."[4]

In effect, closed questions raise salience. This becomes the obvious purpose of many closed questions which are prefaced by a long explanation of the issues presented by the question. For example, the following is a typical attempt not to bias by insuring that all respondents are ostensibly on an equal knowledge footing:

> An increasing number of countries who do not have enough energy are turning to nuclear power as a major source of energy. However, only

3. R. Gary Bridge et al., "Interviewing Changes Attitudes—Sometimes," *Public Opinion Quarterly*, Spring 1977, p. 56.
4. Ibid., p. 63.

a few countries in the world have the technical know-how to build nuclear power plants. The new Carter Administration is worried that if too many countries have nuclear power plants, they can convert that nuclear know-how into producing atom bombs. Do you approve or disapprove the building of nuclear power plants in countries that don't have them now?[5]

Under the guise of not biasing the results, the researcher systematically introduces bias by educating all respondents and then treating all answers as equal, when they in fact are not. Furthermore, by forcing the respondent to answer closed questions with prescribed answer categories, the researcher evades the problem of dealing with the 70 percent of respondents who frankly don't give a damn. No wonder reliance upon this kind of poll data is so hazardous, and skepticism about the survey profession overall is increasing.

Further evidence of the importance of differential weights in treating respondent answers comes from election polling, which has become very accurate compared with other social issue polling. Political pollers know and admit that election outcomes reside in the huge number of uncommitted or uninvolved voters. Only die-hard party workers and very committed party members know who they are going to vote for, routinely vote in elections, and cannot easily be swayed in their decisions. It is the uncommitted voter who can be swayed by charm and bunches of wavy brown hair on the TV screen, or who will switch a vote because of a social gaffe publicly uttered by a candidate from a railroad station or airport runway. No survey can indeed measure whether the uncommitted voter will care enough about this particular election to bother to vote at all. Therefore, political polls attempt to probe the likelihood of voting first by asking about past voting behavior and intensity of feelings about candidates, then by asking about intensity of feelings about issues, and finally by asking about the likelihood of actually voting in the upcoming election.

Compare this in-depth exploration of uncommitted voters with routine social interest and many marketing surveys that rarely pursue the problem of intensity of feeling. For example, a typical poll asked, "How serious do you feel the energy shortage is here in the U.S.—very serious, only somewhat serious, or not

5. Connie DeBoer, "The Polls: Nuclear Energy," *Public Opinion Quarterly*, Fall 1977, p. 406.

serious at all?"[6] This question appears to measure intensity, but in fact we need the following information to determine what level of intensity is being revealed by the respondent:

1) Respondent definitions of his own rating of serious— "What does the word 'serious' or 'shortage' mean to you?"

2) Respondent knowledge of an energy shortage. What is a shortage, upon what facts does the respondent base his opinion that there is or is not a shortage? Has he had trouble getting gas? Has he been unable to heat his home?

The polling business, as a social science, suffers from a mental approach that works for physical science investigation, that is, the idea of a constant in nature. The physical sciences predicate that such a constant exists, and the scientific task is to locate it. The social sciences cannot do this. Certainly, pollers should not make this assumption. If a researcher insists that such a constant exists—that every respondent has a solid point of view and all the researcher must do is locate it—he will deliberately falsify his data. Surveys that refuse to deal with the fact that there is often nothing there fail to provide the information their clients need and are paying for.

Combining open and closed questions

The most obvious solution to identification of respondent meaning, to dealing with the unequal importance of respondent answers, is to use open-ended and closed questions in immediate combination. The closed questions give the statistical count, and the open-ended questions give the meaning of the statistical count.

Here are some very simple but effective ways to use this one-two combination. As discussed earlier, in the abortion study a closed question concerning favorability toward abortion was followed immediately by the open-ended question, "Under what circumstances, if any, would you allow legal abortions?" In a study of organization membership the closed question was, "How would you rate the competence of your chapter leader-

6. Ibid., p. 402.

ship—very good, fairly good, fairly poor, or very poor?" It was followed by, "Why do you say that?" In a bank trust study the closed question was, "Who would you personally be most likely to choose as the executor of your will?" It was followed by, "Why would you choose that person/organization for your executor? PROBE: What were your most important considerations?" In a bank retail study of NOW accounts the closed question was, "Keeping in mind the possible service charges and the minimum balance requirements, overall, how interested would you be in opening an interest-bearing checking account?" The open-ended question that followed was, "Why do you say that?"

The coded answers to the open-ended questions are always analyzed by cross-tabulating the preceding answers to the closed questions. Then these answers are broken out by important demographic variables. Thus, we can define what people mean when they say they are "very favorable," and we can then see if the definitions attached to "very favorable" vary by important subgroups. Usually, astonishingly different meanings for the same words show up by key demographic subgroups, as discussed in the next chapter in regard to generic words.

One final example of the importance of closed and open questions in combination with questions regarding actual behavior rather than only attitude will illustrate the importance of designing the questionnaire as a totality rather than as a bunch of questions. In a study of homeowner's insurance in a large city among inner-city ghetto residents, the basic research problem concerned the issue of "redlining" and the difficulty faced by inner-city residents in obtaining homeowner's insurance. When people were asked, "How easy would you say it is to find the type of home insurance you want—is it very easy, somewhat easy, somewhat difficult, or very difficult to find home insurance?", substantial numbers answered that it was "very difficult" to find homeowner's insurance. People were then asked the follow-up question, "Why do you say that?" Answers included the following:

"Because certain companies don't like to insure certain neighborhoods."

"Because of the area—some people have a hard time getting insurance because of the neighborhood."

"People around the area have said it's difficult. It is a changing area."

"Everyone's having trouble. If you have a fire in your house, the insurance company wants to drop you."

"Well, it is hard for a black person to get insurance in my neighborhood. That's why I said that. That's all."

"I hear people complain. I don't know why they say it's difficult to get insurance."

"Insurance companies will not insure inner-city homes."

"They don't like to give blacks homeowner's insurance, for reasons I don't want to go into."

"In this area a lot of people don't qualify because of the area."

All respondents were asked if they personally had home-owner's insurance and how much difficulty they had actually experienced in obtaining it for themselves. Although people believed it was very difficult to get insurance, in fact most people had obtained the insurance they wanted with relatively little difficulty. Thus, if *only* the attitude question had been asked without the follow-up question, which indicated that much of the perception of difficulty was based on hearsay, the recommendations to the client would have been vastly different. Recommendations would have included greater effort to *provide* insurance to counter criticisms of redlining. Instead, the recommendations to the client emphasized the need for education to change the perceptions of residents, which were not borne out by the facts. These perceptions were detrimental to the community itself, as well as to the insurance industry.

☐ 14
Question wording

My purpose in this chapter on question wording is primarily to emphasize and expand upon the importance of certain types of question approaches. For a more detailed discussion of specific techniques and problems of question wording, the reader is referred to *The Art of Asking Questions*, by Stanley Payne,[1] or to various other books on general survey techniques.

Single-issue questions

Perhaps the most basic principle of question wording, and one very often ignored or simply unseen, is that only *one* concept or issue or meaning should be included in a question. Multiple concepts per question mean that you, the researcher, do not really know which concept the respondent is answering or referring to. If the respondent should somehow meld the multiple concepts into one concept that he is responding to, you will still have no idea of what that concept is. You and the respondent have no common reference point, since you are interpreting the question differently from one another. The answer to a multiple-concept question can refer either to only one of the concepts or to a new concept unstated by either the respondent or the researcher but existing in the respondent's head. In either case the actual answer

1. Stanley Payne, *The Art of Asking Questions* (Princeton, N.J.: Princeton University Press, 1951).

is not accurate because it does not reflect the respondent's true feelings or attitudes or knowledge of the total *stated* question presented to him by the interviewer.

Multiple concepts per question can be either stated explicitly or implied simply by an unfortunate choice of words. I have listed below several questions that have actually been asked in surveys. They are examples of how not to formulate questions if you are seriously interested in answers from your respondent that you can unequivocally interpret and analyze.

1) "How likely would you be to vote for someone who was young and never held office before?"

2) "How likely would you be to vote for someone who was young, who had grown up in New Jersey, who had worked in Washington, but who came back to New Jersey to run for local office?"

3) "Do you believe the U.S. should go ahead and construct the B-1 bomber, the cruise missile, and the new Trident missile submarine?"

4) "Do you agree or disagree with the statement that the ERA is bad because it would encourage women to get jobs and leave their families and homes?"

5) "Considering all the money you pay out in taxes, through such things as income taxes, sales taxes, and property taxes, do you think you are paying too much for what the government at all levels provides in return, too little, or about the right amount?"

6) "Do you favor or oppose the proposed transportation bond issue to build new highways and repair existing highways in the state?"

7) "What problems facing your neighborhood, community, or municipality are you personally most concerned about?"

8) "All things considered, what do you like best about living where you now live?"

Now for the interpretation of these questions.

Question 1. The two concepts in this question are those of youth and inexperience. The respondent may wish to vote for someone who is young but who has experience; or he may wish to vote for someone who is old but is inexperienced. He must make a choice of emphasis in his answer to this question, if he holds either view. How will you know whether he is responding to the issue of age or to the issue of experience? In a political campaign this can be a crucial distinction in the media presentations.

Question 2. This question contains four concepts: youth, grown up in New Jersey, worked in Washington, came back to New Jersey. A respondent may respond favorably to concepts one and two, and negatively to the idea of someone who has worked in Washington coming back to New Jersey. Again, the respondent will either respond to one or two of the concepts, ignoring the rest, or he will reformulate the concepts into a new one in his head that subsumes all of the above. In either event, the researcher cannot know which concepts dominate and influence the respondent the most.

Question 3. The respondent may favor the B-1 bomber but not the other two. How will the researcher know which is the case?

Question 4. The respondent may disagree that the ERA is bad because it encourages women to get jobs, but he may agree that it is bad because women would leave their families and homes. Getting a job is not synonymous with leaving one's family, as most working men and women would agree. What does "leave" mean in this instance? Does it mean leave the family on a daily basis by sending the kids to a baby-sitter? Does it mean abandonment or desertion? The respondent may think it is great that his wife can go out and get a job as a result of the ERA, but he might object if it provokes his wife into abandoning him. How can he answer this question intelligently?

Question 5. While this question has broken the types of taxes into some sort of categories that could imply national (income taxes) versus local (sales and property taxes), the rest of the question deals only with one "government." This question has implied multiple concepts. Although only one government is stipulated, the respondent may quite reasonably think his local government is doing very well for his tax dollars, but that national government is doing poorly, or vice versa. How can he answer this question, and how can the researcher intelligently interpret the answers? While three levels of taxes are mentioned, three levels of government are implied. A separate question about each form of government should be asked to get an intelligent answer that the researcher can analyze with confidence.

Question 6. This question was mentioned earlier in this book. It contains two concepts: repair of existing highways and construction of new highways. As discussed earlier, respondents preferred repair and rejected new construction in an actual bond issue test.

Question 7. This question consists of three concepts or levels of problems: neighborhood, community, and municipality. The respondent might be very concerned about litter in his neighborhood, lack of police protection in his community, and environmental pollution in his municipality. Also, what is the distinction between community and municipality? How are they defined? Even if the respondent lists all three answers separately, the researcher cannot analyze them rationally, because he cannot know to which one of the three civic organizations the answers refer.

Question 8. This question contains an implied multiple concept in the words, "where you now live." Does the researcher mean the respondent's community, state, block, or house? The respondent may like the good streets and highways, the types of housing available, the low school taxes, or the lack of air pollution. If the researcher is asking this question for policymakers at any one of the above three levels—community, state, or neighborhood—he will not be able to distinguish what the respondent's answers mean by referring back, since he cannot know which one of the three levels implied in "where you live" the respondent actually had in mind when answering this question.

In summary, the most important principle of question wording is to treat only one discrete idea or concept per question. Only in this way can you be sure that both you and your respondent have exactly the same issue or problem in mind. You and your respondent will have reached the first level of good communication: you will both know exactly what you are referring to, you in your question and the respondent in his answer.

Generic words

Another problem with multiple concepts per question is the problem of generic words. Many words routinely used in questionnaire design contain multiple meanings, and often meanings that are mutually exclusive or even contradictory. For example, the word "strike" can refer to a labor relations quarrel, to someone who hits another person, or to a baseball game. Unless you ask the respondent to define what he means by his use of a specific generic word, you cannot know what his answer means, or that you and he share the same definition.

I became involved in the problem of generic words through my political research. In one study I asked people to list those qualities they thought most important in a politician. One of the most frequently mentioned answers was "honesty." Then I asked respondents to give examples of "honest" politicians. It was not uncommon to have respondents answer, "Truman and Gold-water." Philosophically, I could see little in common between these two men or some of the other pairs of examples volunteered by respondents. So I asked the respondents to define what they meant by "honesty" in a politician. I obtained at least four major definitions of honesty, and some of them were absolutely contradictory. In addition, the definitions clustered by the political traditions of the communities of the respondents. Thus, in Hudson County, New Jersey, scene of one of the state's most powerful existing political machines, honesty means, "He votes the way I do." In Princeton, a community dominated by old-style liberal politics and a strong sense of noblesse oblige, honesty means, "He votes his conscience." In some communities of the state honesty means, "He is not on the take, not taking bribes." In other areas honesty means, "He tells the truth, tells it like it is."

This experience in attempting to understand political motivations and meaning prompted me to look closely at what I have come to call "generic" words: words with broad meanings. Generic words appear to be universally interpreted in the same way, but in fact they are interpreted in widely different ways by important clusters and subgroups of the general public.

I next tried this technique of asking the respondent to define generic words in another political study. The generic word was "moderate." I found that, to some people, moderate means holding balanced opinions, weighing each side of an issue. To some people, moderate means "a chicken," someone who is afraid to commit himself. To others, moderate means not extreme in his political views, middle of the road.

I used this approach in a bank marketing study concerned with the problem of quality. What makes a quality bank? So I asked people, "What makes this bank outstanding in its 'quality'?" The answers were distributed as follows:

"Quality means a specific bank service (overdraft checking, checking accounts, savings certificates, and so forth)."

"Quality means free checking accounts are provided."

"Quality means the tellers and bank personnel are friendly, polite, courteous, cheerful."

"Quality means that bank personnel have a personal interest in customers. They know you by your name and give you very personalized service."

"Quality means that you never have mistakes on your statements, no errors."

"Quality means good location and convenient hours when the bank is open."

Another very common generic word used in bank marketing studies, and also in many other marketing studies, is "convenience." What does convenience mean to you? Convenience as applied to banking means variously:

"The bank is located close to my home."

"The bank is open Saturdays, nights, and evenings."

"The bank provides a lot of different services—all the services needed—under one roof."

"The bank has a drive-in window, automatic teller machines."

"It is easy to cash checks, no lines, no hassles, no errors."

I have continued to use this technique of definition of generic words in many other studies with stunning results in obtaining greater understanding and depth of respondent answers and consequent respondent behavior. The words, "family planning," for example, mean birth control to a majority of people, but to an important minority they mean financial planning for the future and getting together to do things as a family. Interestingly, men are somewhat more likely to think in terms of financial planning than birth control, a subtle indicator that birth control is still seen as mainly a woman's problem.

Generic words dominate surveys and contribute to the lack of certainty with which data can be interpreted and acted upon. "Would you say that you got enough exercise at the present time or not?" What is the meaning of the word "exercise"? "Aside from any work you do here at home or at a job, do you do anything regularly—that is on a daily basis—that helps you keep physically fit?" How do respondents define "physically fit"? What does it mean to them?

A very important generic word commonly used is "profit." People are asked what percentage of corporate profits manufacturing companies routinely earn. Yet we have no indication that people accurately define profit, which is so crucial in affecting their attitudes. Jaynes argues in his book, and others have also, that unless you can put a word to it, you cannot think it. I argue further that unless a respondent can define it, he cannot know it, and if he defines it differently from me, I cannot know what he thinks unless I ask him.

Wording of open-ended questions

I have discussed the ways that open-ended questions provide insight into respondent meaning and definition of issues. The same problems of question wording (use of simple, understandable words, employing only a single concept per question, stating implied alternatives, and so forth) that apply to closed questions also apply to open-ended questions. With wording of open questions, particular care must be used to define accurately the dimension or concept that you want the respondent to deal with, or the respondent will give you a poor answer.

As an example of poor wording of open-ended questions, the following questions were asked of people who said that they had set up a trust, either for themselves or for someone else:

1) "What were your most important purposes for setting up this trust/these trusts?"

2) "What factors in your personal situation made setting up a trust particularly desirable for you?"

The first question was intended to obtain the respondent's reasons or goals in setting up the trust. In fact, respondents answered this question very well. Answers fell into categories dealing with protection of dependents, insuring orderly distribution of assets, insuring competent handling of assets by professional managers, and so forth.

The second question was aimed at learning what specific factors in the respondent's personal situation made a trust appear to be a good solution. Respondents essentially answered this question with goals rather than a description of their personal situation. Personal situation answers were occasionally given, such as personal tax situation, ownership of a business, or existence of a mentally incompetent minor, but, by and large, answers to this question were redundant with answers to the preceding one.

□ 15
Summary

Rather than just a series of questions lumped together on a page, a questionnaire consists of the following layers of approach and method:

1) Hypotheses, which act as the foundation and guide for all individual questions to be included.

2) Question routing to encourage respondent cooperation, aid flow, and prevent mind sets, particularly position effect.

3) Leading the respondent: introducing knowledge and testing its effects on respondent attitudes.

4) Questions in three important areas: structures and environment, knowledge, and actual behavior.

5) Sequencing of questions and construction of series of questions to help identify levels of respondent consciousness.

6) Question formulation: closed, multiple choice, free response, and open with precoded response.

7) Question formulation to insure that only one issue is included per question.

8) Question formulation to identify dimensions of issues, to obtain respondent definition of terms, and to measure levels of respondent consciousness.

9) Wording of questions: generic, ambiguous, and biased words.

10) Formatting for keypunching, tabulation, and interviewer comprehension.

Sample questionnaire

To give greater visual expression to these different layers of questionnaire design, on the following pages I present a draft questionnaire dealing with issues related to wills and estates. For each page of the questionnaire, I will point out the layers represented by each question, which will in turn demonstrate the interlocking nature of these layers within any questionnaire; that is, each layer cannot be dealt with separately. All layers must be dealt with comprehensively and simultaneously, keeping in mind the ultimate analytical procedures to be used on the data.

Hypotheses—goals of the study

The trust department of a major bank commissioned a marketing study of present trust customers of the client bank and other banks, and of potential trust customers, defined as those people who have a will or who have enough assets to justify a trust.

The basic hypotheses underlying this study were that:

1) If people knew the complexities involved, they would ask professionals to act as executors rather than friends or family.

2) If people knew anything about probate laws in the state, they would be more likely to draw up a will.

3) People really don't understand how large their estates can become if life insurance and mortgage-free homes are included.

Additional hypotheses relating to subsequent data analysis were used to draw out answers to the basic hypotheses listed above. These more specific hypotheses are listed for each appropriate question.

Formatting

All answer categories are on the right side for ease of location by interviewer and keypuncher. All interviewer instructions are located on the questionnaire at each appropriate question. The interviewer does not need to refer back to preceding pages.

Question wording

For many of the open-ended questions, I have deliberately used multiple meanings to provoke the respondent to give a deeper answer. For the closed questions, I have tried to use only one concept per question.

Page 1 of questionnaire

TIME INTERVIEW BEGUN _____

INTERVIEWING LOCATION _____

Hello, my name is _____ and I am calling for R L Associates of Princeton, New Jersey. We are interviewing people about their familiarity with different types of bank *trust* services.

I'd like to speak with the person in your household who would have the most responsibility for handling your wills and your household's financial planning.

1. Respondent is:

> 1 MALE
> 2 FEMALE

2. I'd like to begin by asking you a few questions about your family. . .

    What is your marital status?

> 1 MARRIED
> 2 DIVORCED, WIDOWED
> 3 SEPARATED
> 4 SINGLE, NEVER MARRIED

3. How many adults, over age 21, live in your household?

> 1 ONE
> 2 TWO
> 3 THREE
> 4 FOUR OR MORE

4. How many children, if any, under age 21 do you have basic financial responsibility for?

> 1 ONE
> 2 TWO
> 3 THREE
> 4 FOUR OR MORE
> 5 NONE

5. Do you presently have a legal will?

> 1 YES–**GO TO Q.12**
> 2 NO

Questions 1,2,3,4

Hypotheses: (1) current family structure determines or influences people's perceived need for a will; (2) financial responsibility for children influences people's perceived need for a will.

Routing: begin with some relevant demographics. If respondent terminates later in the interview, we can then analyze nonrespondents compared to respondents on these sensitive issues.

Question 5

Structure and environment: type of household/family.

Routing: this question acts as a filter or screen to divide respondents into two groups—those with wills and those without.

Behavior: this is a basic behavior question that can be analyzed by key demographics to determine differences, if any, between those people with wills and those without.

Page 2 of questionnaire

IF "NO," ASK:

6. What are the most important reasons why you do not have a will at this time?

7. Thinking of yourself personally, if you were to die now, what would be your primary concern about the handling or distribution of your estate?

8. As far as you know, what are the most important tasks performed by the executor of a will—that is, the person or organization who carries out the instructions of your will?

9. Who would you personally be most likely to choose as the executor of your will if you had one?

       1   F R I E N D
       2   WIFE, HUSBAND
         3   OTHER RELATIVE
         4   LAWYER
           5   ACCOUNTANT
           6   BANK
           7   OTHER _____
           8   DON'T KNOW—GO TO
                             Q. 25

10. Why would you choose that person/organization for your executor? PROBE: What were your most important considerations?

Questions 6,7

Hypotheses: people do not have wills because:

   a) they say they do not have enough estate to warrant it.

   b) they think they do not have time to do it.

   c) they simply have not thought about it or become conscious of the need.

   d) they don't see a need (are single, no children, etc.).

   e) they do not feel they can afford lawyer's fees.

   f) other reasons that we have not anticipated.

Consciousness: answers will indicate depth of respondent consciousness about need for a will.

Question 8

Hypothesis: people really don't know what executors do; therefore, they do not think an executor need be an expert.

Consciousness: how much have they thought about what executors do?

Knowledge: what do they actually know about the tasks involved?

Question 9

Question formulation: attitude, open with precoded answer categories.

Hypothesis: people will usually choose friends or relations as their executors.

Routing: "Don't know" screened out of subsequent series because of lack of conscious involvement in idea of a will and/or executor.

Question 10

Hypotheses: (1) people choose friends or relatives because they think these people know them so well personally that they will do the best job of administering the will; (2) people choose friends and family to avoid lawyer's fees.

Consciousness: how much have people actually thought about their choice? Meaning of respondent selection in Question 9.

Page 3 of questionnaire

IF "BANK" NOT MENTIONED IN Q.9 ASK:

11. Why wouldn't you choose a bank to act as executor of your will?

GO TO Q. 17

IF "YES," HAVE A WILL ON Q. 5, ASK:

12. What were the most important reasons why you decided to write a will? PROBE: What did you want to accomplish with your will?

13. As far as you know, what are the most important tasks performed by the executor of a will—that is, the person or organization who carries out the instructions of your will?

14. Who did you choose to be the executor of your will? (Read categories below.)

> 1 FRIEND
> 2 WIFE, HUSBAND
> 3 OTHER RELATIVE
> 4 LAWYER
> 5 ACCOUNTANT
> 6 BANK
> 7 OTHER _____
> 8 DON'T KNOW—GO TO Q. 24

15. Why did you choose that person/organization for your executor? PROBE: What were your most important considerations?

Question 11

Hypothesis: people can't give any reason for not considering a bank.

Consciousness: have they thought about it at all?

Knowledge: do they know anything about what a bank does or could do?

Routing: screen out those who do not have a will from subsequent questions asked of those who do have a will.

Questions 12,13

Hypotheses: (1) concern over children prompted writing of will; (2) concern over spouse prompted writing of will; (3) people felt wealthy enough that they needed a will.

Consciousness: have they thought about it?

Knowledge: what do they know about wills; what do they do?

Question 14

Same as Question 9.

Question 15

Same as Question 10.

Page 4 of questionnaire

IF "BANK" NOT MENTIONED IN Q. 14 ABOVE, ASK:

16. Why didn't you choose a bank to act as executor of your will?

ASK EVERYONE:

17. I am going to read you a series of items. Please tell me how important *each* item would be to you in the handling of your will and your estate. Would it be very important, fairly important, or not too important to you?

		Very Impor- tant	Fairly Impor- tant	Not Too Impor- tant	Don't Know
a.	A good knowledge of accounting.	1	2	3	4
b.	A good knowledge of federal income tax laws.	1	2	3	4
c.	A good knowledge of court procedures in the probate of wills.	1	2	3	4
d.	A good knowledge of your personal affairs and your personal wishes.	1	2	3	4
e.	A good knowledge of real estate and invest- ment procedures to protect your assets while they are being distributed.	1	2	3	4

18. Thinking of the person you have selected/would select as your executor, how would you rate him/her on knowledge of accounting—excellent, good, fair, or poor?

1 EXCELLENT
2 GOOD
3 FAIR
4 POOR
5 DON'T KNOW

19. As far as you know, has that person ever taken any courses in accounting?

1 YES
2 NO
3 DON'T KNOW

Question 16

Same as Question 11.

Questions 17, 18, 19

Leading: multidimensional issues. Ask how important each item is to respondent. Distributed answers will give ranks to each task of executor. Differences in these ratings of importance, analyzed by demographics, will give some idea of what marketing themes will appeal most to different demographic subgroups.

Consciousness: this entire sequence may result in logical inconsistencies between what the respondent says is important to him in an executor and his actual choice of an executor; that is, if only importance is asked alone, we may take his answers at face value, whereas follow-up on the qualifications of his own choice of an executor may confirm or deny the meaningfulness of his answers on Question 17.

Question formulation: standard simple scaling technique.

Page 5 of questionnaire

20. Thinking of the person you have selected/would select as your executor, how would you rate him/her on knowledge of federal income tax laws—excellent, good, fair, or poor?

        1 EXCELLENT
        2 GOOD
        3 FAIR
        4 POOR
        5 DON'T KNOW

21. As far as you know, has that person ever taken any courses on tax law?

        1 YES
        2 NO
        3 DON'T KNOW

22. How would you rate this person on knowledge of court probate procedures—excellent, good, fair, or poor?

        1 EXCELLENT
        2 GOOD
        3 FAIR
        4 POOR
        5 DON'T KNOW

23. Does this person have a law degree?

        1 YES
        2 NO
        3 DON'T KNOW

ASK EVERYONE:

24. I am going to read you a series of statements. For each one, please tell me whether you basically agree or disagree.

		Agree	Disagree	Don't Know
a.	A married man/woman who owns everything in joint names does not need a will.	1	2	3
b.	If a married *woman* without children dies without a will, her husband will receive part of her estate, and her *parents* will receive part.	1	2	3
c.	A *widow* will have to prove to the Internal Revenue Service that she has paid for her share of a joint estate; otherwise, she will have to pay taxes on all of it.	1	2	3

Questions 20,21,22,23

Leading: multidimensional issues. Ask how important each item is to respondent. Distributed answers will give ranks to each task of executor. Differences in these ratings of importance, analyzed by demographics, will give some idea of what marketing themes will appeal most to different demographic subgroups.

Consciousness: this entire sequence may result in logical inconsistencies between what the respondent says is important to him in an executor and his actual choice of an executor: that is, if only importance is asked alone, we may take his answers at face value, whereas follow-up on the qualifications of his own choice of an executor may confirm or deny the meaningfulness of his answers on Question 17.

Question formulation: standard simple scaling technique.

Question 24

Knowledge

Page 6 of questionnaire

25. Have you personally ever acted as an executor of someone's will?

        1 YES
        2 NO

26. Have you ever known anyone personally who had acted as executor of someone's will?

        1 YES
        2 NO

27. Last year, did you use a professional accountant to prepare your personal income tax return?

        1 YES
        2 NO

28. Have you ever set up a trust for yourself or someone else?

        1 YES
        2 NO

IF "YES," SET UP TRUST, ASK:

29. For whom did you set up that trust—yourself, your spouse, your children, or some other person?

        1 SELF
        2 SPOUSE
        3 CHILDREN
        4 OTHER

Question 25
Behavior

Question 26
Knowledge

Question 27
Behavior
Consciousness: confirms or denies level of importance attached to taxes and accounting in Question 17.

Question 28
Behavior
Routing: screens out all nonqualified respondents from next section on trusts.

Question 29
Behavior

This sample questionnaire makes it clear that the development of such an instrument demands attention not only to wording problems, but also to the integration of those carefully chosen words into questions, which are in turn ordered within the questionnaire to provide greater understanding of respondent meaning. All of these questionnaire techniques are used as a means of testing hypotheses formulated to solve real problems for clients.

While I would be the last to argue that the tasks outlined in this book are easy, or that I successfully accomplish them in every questionnaire I write, I can only encourage questionnaire writers and their clients to persist, because the great depth, insight, and richness of the data obtained from a well-constructed questionnaire provide the real pleasure involved in survey research.

Bibliography

American Institute of Public Opinion. *The Gallup Poll.* Vol. III, 1959–1971. New York: Random House, 1972.

———————. *The Gallup Poll.* Vol. I, 1972–1975. Wilmington, Delaware: Scholarly Resources, Inc., 1978.

Becker, Ernest. *The Denial of Death.* New York: The Free Press, Macmillan, 1973.

Benedict, Ruth. *Patterns of Culture.* Boston: Houghton Mifflin, Sentry Edition, 1961.

Bradburn, Norman. *The Structure of Psychological Well-Being.* Chicago: Aldine, 1969.

Braudel, Fernand. *The Mediterranean and the Mediterranean World in the Age of Philip II.* 2 vols. New York: Harper & Row, 1972.

Bridge, R. Gary et al. "Interviewing Changes Attitudes—Sometimes." *Public Opinion Quarterly,* Spring 1977: 56–64.

DeBoer, Connie. "The Polls: Nuclear Energy." *Public Opinion Quarterly,* Fall 1977.

Dillman, Don A. *Mail and Telephone Surveys.* New York: John Wiley & Sons, 1978.

Jaynes, Julian. *The Origin of Consciousness in the Breakdown of the Bicameral Mind.* Boston: Houghton Mifflin, 1976.

Lee, Robert S. "Social Attitudes and the Computer Revolution." *Public Opinion Quarterly,* Spring 1970: 53–59.

Maddi, Salvatore R. *Personality Theories, A Comparative Analysis.* Homewood, Illinois: The Dorsey Press, 1968.

May, Rollo. *Love and Will.* New York: W. W. Norton, 1969.

Payne, Stanley L. *The Art of Asking Questions.* Princeton, New Jersey: Princeton University Press, 1951.

Petersen, William. *Population.* 3rd ed. New York: Macmillan, 1975.

Pezzullo, Mary Ann. "Quantifying Quality." Prepared by R L Associates for United Jersey Banks (Princeton, New Jersey), 1978.

Rappeport, Michael. "The Distinction the Pollsters Don't Make." *The Washington Monthly*, March 1974: 13–15.

Rappeport, Michael and Labaw, Patricia. "Abortion as a National Issue." Prepared by R L Associates for the Planned Parenthood Federation of America, Inc., 1979.

_____. "1978–1979 Title XX Human Services Needs Assessment Study." Prepared by R L Associates for the Office of Policy and Management, Connecticut Department of Human Resources, 1979.

_____. "The Public Evaluates the NIAAA Public Education Campaign." Prepared by Opinion Research Corporation for the Alcohol, Drug Abuse, and Mental Health Administration, Public Health Service, U. S. Department of Health, Education, and Welfare, July 1975.

Rokeach, Milton. "Attitude Change and Behavioral Change." *Public Opinion Quarterly*, Winter 1966–1967: 29–50.

Roshco, Bernard. "The Polls: Polling on Panama." *Public Opinion Quarterly*, Winter 1978.

United States District Court. Southern District of New York. *Charles Revson, Inc., Plaintiff, Against Max Factor & Co., Defendant.* August 3, 1977.

Index